YESTERDAY,
TODAY
AND FOREVER

Maria von Trapp

YESTERDAY, TODAY AND FOREVER

NEW LEAF PRESS

Harrison, Arkansas

First Printing, Casebound, June 1975
Second Printing, Casebound, October 1975
Third Printing, Casebound, February 1976
Fourth Printing, Casebound, January 1977
Fifth Printing, Paperback, February 1977
Sixth Printing, Paperback, October 1977
Seventh Printing, Paperback, November 1978
Eighth Printing, Paperback, January 1980
Ninth Printing, Paperback, January 1981

Portions of this book are from a book published in 1952 by J.B. Lippincott Company, *Yesterday, Today, and Forever.*

CONTENTS

how it happened   9

ONE
YESTERDAY

1. "in those days"   17
2. Palestine in winter   19
3. "Away in a manger"   23
4. "Silent Night, Holy Night"   27
5. "Angels we Have Heard on High"   29
6. Mary pondered in her heart   34
7. candlemas day   39
8. Caspar, Melchior, and Balthasar   51
9. the fugitive   66
10. "unless you . . . become as little children"   76
11. "Did you not know . . . ?"   86
12. the carpenter   98
13. the Son of Man   102

a word in between   105

TWO
TODAY

14.	"the other cheek"	111
15.	"I have called you friends"	118
16.	"He . . . healed them"	127
17.	"and certain women . . . ministered unto Him"	132
18.	"a woman clothed with the sun . . ."	141
19.	today	145
20.	a letter	148

THREE
FOREVER

21.	blessed are the dead	161
22.	the judgement	164
23.	"Begone, Satan!"	169
24.	"eye hath not seen"	172

YESTERDAY,
TODAY
AND FOREVER

how it happened

It was in Italian South Tyrol in a primitive little country inn on the edge of a lovely village in the mountains. The year was 1938, and this was the first station on our flight from Nazi-invaded Austria. We, that is, Father Wasner, my husband and I, and nine children with the tenth on the way, had just barely arrived at this peaceful little place when it happened. With a terrific wail, Lorli, aged six, discovered that we had forgotten her favorite toy, a worn-out, shapeless, hairless something, formerly a teddy bear.

The grief of a child is always terrible. It is bottomless, without hope. A child has no past and no future. It just lives in the present moment—wholeheartedly. If the present moment spells disaster, the child suffers it with his whole heart, his whole soul, his whole strength, his whole little being; and because a child is so helpless in his grief, we should never take it lightly, but drop all we are doing at the moment and come to his aid.

I remember the situation so well, the glassed-in veranda in which we were standing, and me looking for a cookie or a candy, and there was none. Had I forgotten that we were refugees now, and luxuries like candies were things of the past? But even if the hands of a mother are empty, her mind and heart must never be. Taking the sobbing little girl on my lap, I said: "Come, Lorli, Mother is going to tell you a story."

That had always worked; but now it only brought forth new tears, and violently shaking her little head with its mop of dark curls, she shrieked, "I don't want to hear about Cinderella or Snow White—I want . . ."

"Oh no, Lorli," I said, "I'm not going to tell you one of those stories; but if you will listen to me, I will tell you the story of another Child like you to Whom the same thing happened—oh, a wonderful story!" And as I said this, I had no idea of what I was going to tell.

"Once upon a time," I began, "there was a mother, a father, and a little Child."

"A girl?" Lorli managed to ask between sobs.

"No, a Boy," I said.

At this very moment I saw them right before me, the Holy Family on their way to Egypt. For the first time, however, I didn't think of them the way the holy cards pictured them—Mary in blue, Joseph in brown, the little Child in pink, each one with a golden hem on his garment—riding complacently on a neat donkey through a beautiful countryside full of date palms. For the first time it dawned on me that they were really refugees like millions of people nowadays, like ourselves, for instance.

"Flee," said the angel to Joseph, "flee into Egypt, for Herod will seek the Child to destroy Him."

Wasn't the fright which must have chilled Joseph's blood at that moment, the same fright which we had experienced so often when we heard the cruel stories of how the Gestapo was on somebody's heels, how they had dragged away fathers or brothers from families we knew? Wasn't it the same fright which had finally gotten us across the border? The angel had not announced to Joseph just exactly what Herod intended to do, but Joseph knew that Herod's Gestapo worked fast, and that his reputation for cruelty was unequaled. If the parents wanted to save the Child, they had to hurry to get away from Herod; and while I told my little girl the story of the Flight into Egypt, I listened to it myself. It was so new, so not at all holy-card-wise. It was so excitingly modern, the story of refugees, who, after having reached the goal, Egypt, became displaced persons, D.P.'s. It was a story full of anxiety and homesickness, but also full of trust in the Heavenly Father, Who in His own good time, provides a home for all refugees.

Lorli had long since stopped crying. In rapt attention she listened to my description of the dangers of the flight. I told about the wild animals and robbers, the terrific heat at noon and the cold at night on that dangerous passage through the desert, which even the Roman soldiers dreaded, and how the little Boy did not make any fuss over missing a toy, not once.

Then the angel of the Lord appeared again to Joseph, in my story, and bade him to return home.

"Will an angel tell our father, too, when we can go back to Salzburg?" asked Lorli eagerly.

"Yes," I said without the slightest hesitation, and a happy little girl glided down from my lap and ran off to Stefan, the innkeeper's little boy, to tell him this, her newest story.

Some of the older children had moved over from the other side of the veranda during the story.

"Mother, that was really exciting," they said. I was completely taken with it myself. During the telling it had become more and more clear in my own mind: This story isn't over yet. All this is still going on.

"Children," I said, "I feel as though we were at the beginning of a great discovery. It seems as if Herod weren't really dead. He keeps on living under different names, like Saul and Nero, or Hitler and Stalin. He still seeks the Child to destroy Him." How close Our Lord and His family had become all of a sudden when we met them as fellow refugees!

That was a big discovery, and it came to us on the very threshold of a new life when we had joined the millions of refugees on the highways and byways of Europe in search of a new home. But I have told about all this in my other book, *The Story of the Trapp Family Singers,* and I don't want to repeat any of it here. This is to be simply the story of how "Jesus Christ, yesterday, and today, and the same forever" (Heb. 13:8)—finally became a member of our family.

In that summer of our flight through Europe we had another startling experience. It was a few weeks after the in-

cident on the glassed-in veranda. One of our sons was engaged
to be married, and his bride-to-be spent several weeks with
us in Holland. One day she came to me and said:

"Mother, can you tell me what he was like when he was a
baby? He has told me everything about his life as far as he
can remember, but—I want to know all."

That hit me right between the eyes. Reading the Gospels
together and searching in them for more modern stories like
the one of the Flight into Egypt had become a family hobby
by then. Merely by doing it, we had found out how little we
knew about Our Lord and His family, His country and His
times. Aside from stating that fact, we hadn't done anything
about it. Then came this girl who went out of her way to find
out every detail about the one whom she loved because—
"she had to know all." This did something to us.

"How can we pretend to love Our Lord," we said to
ourselves, "if we don't want to know all about Him as
well?"

On that same evening during night prayer it occurred to me
that Mary, the mother of Christ, was a mother like me.
Perhaps she would be just as pleased about the questioning
as I had been, and so I turned to God and said:

"Father, there is so little written in the Gospels about
your Son when He was a Child and while He was growing up.
How was it in Nazareth, in Bethlehem, in Egypt? Was He
lively or was He rather quiet? What did He eat, what did He
wear? What did He do all day long, and you and St. Joseph?"

I don't believe in chances and coincidences. It must have
been she who gave two friends of ours, independently of
each other, the idea to present us with books: *The Life of
Christ* by the German Jesuit, Meschler, and the one by
Mauriac. There could hardly be found a greater contrast than
between those two works on the same subject. That was the
beginning of a very helpful little library of our own. After we
had finished these two books, we wanted to know more. And
more. And more. God has never stopped answering our
questions. Besides helping us to find the right books, He also
helped us to remember what we had once learned in history,
geography, archaeology, and religion. He drew our attention

to the fact that besides the four Canonical Gospels there is something else which we can almost regard as a "fifth Gospel," so much a source of information it is: the Holy Land itself. Very much of it is still exactly the same as it was in His time. There we started getting interested in maps of modern and ancient Palestine.

Many years have passed since. After we had shared with Him the anxiety of the flight, we lived through years of the Hidden Life, and then through the excitement of the Public Life. Many notebooks have been filled with information which we drew out of different books, which seem to complement each other. Pictures of the Holy Land have been cut out of magazines throughout the years, and postal cards sent to us from there by friends have been collected; and putting all these different pieces together is like assembling a crêche.

Every time we say the Creed, we say towards the end that we believe in the Communion of Saints.

Of the early Church it is said: "The multitude of the believers had but one heart and one soul: neither did anyone say that aught of the things which he possessed was his own, but all things were common unto them" (Acts 4:32). That did not refer only to money and the things money can buy, but also and foremost to spiritual goods. We know from the Acts and Epistles of the Apostles and the writings of the early Fathers that this was true. Haven't we moved far away from those times? While we still might share our earthly possessions and contribute to collections, we certainly are not in the habit of sharing our spiritual goods any more. This is our innermost private life, and what I learned this morning in meditation or what occurred to me during reading is nobody's business. This is the spirit of "I—me—myself," whereas the right spirit is always "we—our," as we find in the liturgy, in the prayers of the Church. This would make the difference between a family and a group of people living together under one roof.

It is in this spirit that we want to share with you our great discovery: the bringing of the Holy Scriptures to life for us: and, by watching Him, learning to imitate

Him, learning how to live, how to love, how to die. In the world situation of today it may look like five minutes to twelve, but if we Christians would wake up to the meaning of our name and become "other Christs," we might bring about what was promised only to men of good will: peace on earth.

ONE

YESTERDAY

I

"in those days"

Whenever we read the life story of one of the great ones, be it Washington, Lincoln, Napoleon, or Julius Caesar, we always find that the biographer takes pains to picture for us the time in which his hero lived, thus helping us to understand certain features of his character, certain happenings of his age. So Luke, the biographer of Christ's childhood, does the same.

"In those days," he says, "there went out a decree from Caesar Augustus that the whole world should be enrolled."

"In those days." That means the time when in Rome the nephew of the great Julius Caesar had become emperor. His real name had been Octavius, but his soldiers hailed him as "Augustus." In those days the Roman troops had been victorious almost to the ends of the then-known world. They had invaded country after country in many bloody wars, but now the whole empire was at peace. Before Augustus came into power, terrible civil wars had raged. These and all the invasions had exhausted the finances of the empire, and so Caesar Augustus used this new peace to think of new means to fill the coffers of the state. His new idea was to get every single one of his subjects, without exception, to make a contribution. To help the publicans, or tax collectors, in their business, he ordered now, like the owner of a big department store, an inventory to be made.

"And in those days it came to pass that there went out a decree from Caesar Augustus that the whole world should be enrolled."

"The whole world"—what a proud phrase! But these

were almost the facts. Almost all of what was then known of the world was ruled by Roman governors according to Roman law, and the Roman legions watched on the borders.

In those days one of the more important provinces was Syria, and the official in charge of the census in this province was Quirinius. Tucked away in one corner of his province was a tiny little kingdom of Judea, with Herod as its king.

When Caesar Augustus decided on the census, messengers on horseback galloped along the famous Roman highways carrying the new law north and south. At the same time fast galleys left the Roman ports to take the message across the seas. One of them would arrive in Syria, and Quirinius would sub-delegate King Herod to carry out the census in his land. Herod, who owed his kingship to the Romans, would be only too eager to oblige.

These enrollments were usually made in the places where the people lived. But the Jews had a different custom, and it had always been the policy of the Romans to respect the local habits and customs of conquered nations. Since ancient times the Jews had been divided into tribes. To each tribe belonged a certain county of Palestine with a family headquarters.

St. Joseph belonged to the tribe of Juda and to the house and family of David. The place where David the King had been born and raised was Bethlehem, which later became the headquarters of the House of David. When, therefore, on a certain winter day a messenger came to Nazareth, the little town in Galilee, reading aloud to all the men the imperial decree, "all went to be enrolled, every one into his own city.

And Joseph also went up from Galilee, out of the city of Nazareth into Judea, to the city of David, which is called Bethlehem—because he was, of the house and family of David—to be enrolled with Mary, his espoused wife, who was with child."

II

Palestine in winter

When my husband was still in the Navy, he once spent some time in the Holy Land. It proved to be wonderful for us later.

When, for instance, we wanted to find out about that winter journey of Mary and Joseph from Nazareth to Bethlehem, we simply said, "Tell us, what is the Holy Land like in winter?"

"Oh well," he used to say, "that depends upon where you are. Small as it is, Palestine has three distinct zones. There is that deep gulley, the Jordan Valley, below the level of the Mediterranean. There it is always tropical. Then there are the heights of Mount Hermon, always covered with snow. The weather there I found very much like the Alps. At the same time there is the rather mild climate in the hill country, Galilee, Samaria, and Judea. But why do I say 'mild'?" he corrected himself. "In the winter, that means in the rainy season, it can be simply awful. The rains start in October and last until March. 'It never rains but it pours,' one can really say of those tropical showers. The winds blowing down from the mountains are ice-cold."

"It was about thirty years ago," said my husband meditatively, "when our ship anchored in the Bay of Haifa, and all the officers were invited by some Arab sheik to make a trip on horseback throughout the country. That was before the times of modernization. No bulldozers had yet reached the Holy Land and we were assured time and again that what we saw was pretty much as it had been since time immemorial.

"We were there around Christmastime. The rainy season had been going on for almost three months, and the moment one left the highway, the horse sank in the deep mud. We were astonished to find everywhere the peasants in their fields plowing and sowing, and we asked why they didn't wait for the dry season. But we were told that the sun bakes the earth so terribly that the primitive plows couldn't break the hard soil. I remember we usually saw groups of plowmen working together with their tiny oxen and little plows, merely scratching furrows. We used to stop our horses and watch them for a little while. Often they were shivering in the cold. One old man I remember was holding a basket of seeds, and with tears in his eyes, complained to our interpreter about the weather. When I think of him now in his brown woolen tunic, soaked through and heavy with rain, I can imagine what Saint Joseph must have looked like.''

From there we went on to figure it all out for ourselves: Mary and Joseph locking up their little house in Nazareth and setting out in the rain on their eighty-mile trip. Mary was in no condition to travel. She expected her Child any day now, but obviously the census was meant for men and women alike, and Mary, knowing that the Messiah had to be born in Bethlehem, knew she had to go. They were not rich enough to afford camels, the only convenient way of travel in those days, but they took a donkey. No saddles or stirrups were used at that time. Mary had to sit on a folded blanket laid across the sharp-pointed back of the little animal. How long would it have taken them to reach Bethlehem? From the writings of Julius Caesar we know that the Roman soldiers were supposed to make twenty miles daily when they were not armed, and twelve miles a day under arms. But those were sturdy, strong young men, and here was a young mother expecting her first Child within a few days. She surely couldn't make more than twelve miles a day.

When we, the entire family, traveled all over South America it also happened to be in the winter, in the rainy season. If one was caught in a tropical shower, one was drenched within a few minutes. A few short hours, after

Mary and Joseph had left the houses of Nazareth behind them, the rain must have soaked their woolen mantles and woolen tunics, and the hooves of the little ass spattered mud on them. The garments would never become quite dry until they had reached Bethlehem. Heavier and heavier they would hang on their shoulders as the mud crust became thicker every day.

Such a trip was not without its dangers in those days. Only since the Crusades, in the twelfth century, have lions become extinct in the Holy Land. Throughout Holy Scriptures we find warnings against lions, wolves, and other wild animals. Maybe Mary and Joseph did not always reach an inn, and they had to camp out one or more nights on the roadside. Then a fire had to be made and kept going throughout the night to keep the wild animals away.

There was another pest of the highway—the robbers. The country was infested with them. Large bands of them lived in the hills and threatened the travelers. When we say "inn," we must not think of a comfortable, homey, New England cottage-like building. We mustn't even think of a building at all. The inn by the roadside in the Holy Land consisted usually of a wall twelve to fifteen feet high, surrounding a quadrangle, in the middle of which a big fire was burning. The innkeeper let the travelers in who, for a small payment, could spend the night around the fire unmolested by robbers and wild animals. But they had to provide their own food, and the only comfort was freedom from fear.

Mary and Joseph wound their way slowly down the hills of Galilee through the plains of Estralon towards the hills of Judea. It must have been very hard for Mary to sit for hours at a time with no rest for her back, being bounced by the hard, mincing steps of the little donkey. She might lean on Joseph's shoulder for a little while; he might help her down so she could walk a bit. But wading through the mud didn't help much either, so she would go back to the donkey, always patient, with a weary little smile. But it must have torn Joseph's heart to see her uncomfortable like this, and be unable to do much to help. His whole heart must have been longing for Bethlehem, his home town, where his father's house was still standing and his brothers and kindred were still living. If only they were safe in Bethlehem, then everything would be all right. The family would provide fresh, dry clothing, and in the privacy of her own room, Mary would quickly recover from the hardships of this trip.

These might have been the thoughts of Joseph as he was leading the donkey by the reins up and down the hills through the rain and wind for eight, nine, maybe ten long days, while Mary's heart repeated all over again and again: "Behold the handmaid of the Lord. Be it done to me according to Thy Word."

"But pray that your flight be not in the winter" (Matt. 24:20), Our Lord would admonish His listeners later. It seems that His mother must have told Him about her unforgettable trip from Nazareth to Bethlehem—in the winter.

III

"away in a manger"

"Is it true what Rupert said," asked young Martina woefully, "that in the Holy Land around Christmas it is always warm like in summer, and roses and violets bloom in Bethlehem? On all Christmas cards Bethlehem is deeply covered with snow, and in our Christmas carols it's always a white Christmas, and I like that much better."

"No, it's quite possible that the first Christmas was a white Christmas, too," answered Father Wasner. "In the book of the Machabees it is written: 'But there fell a great snow, and he'—Tryphon—'came not into the country of Galaad' " (I Mac. 13:22).

"And Flavius Josephus, who was a citizen of Jerusalem one generation after Our Lord, says somewhere that in Jericho down at the Jordan there is always a wonderful temperature, that the people there are only dressed in linen, 'even when snow covers the rest of Judea,' " said I, who had gotten a popular edition of the works of Flavius Josephus for Christmas.

Agathe added, "Only recently I read in a book that an officer wrote home that when he came out from Midnight Mass in Bethlehem, he saw snow covering the ground."

Snow or no snow—it doesn't seem so very important, but it certainly was a help to us in picturing Mary and Joseph traveling through the short, cold December days towards Bethlehem. Everybody likes to see his home town again. Last summer when we went back to our home town, Salzburg, in Austria, everyone in the family afterwards confessed the same thing: how his heart was beating faster as the train drew closer; how eagerly he was looking out for the first landmark, the fortress; how he was hoping to find the countryside the way we had left it years ago. And we had an American friend with us, Hester, to whom we now proudly pointed out the sights.

Once outside of Jerusalem, there were only six more miles to go, and Joseph must have glanced eagerly southward to see whether he could see the first familiar landmark, the pillar over Rachel's sepulchre.

"Salzburg is a very old place," we explained with pride to Hester, "fifteen hundred years old."

The same thing Joseph could have said to his bride from the north, because Bethlehem was an old place already when, a thousand years before them, their ancestor David watched the sheep in the fields outside the little town. After five miles the road turns sharply to the east, and there they saw a brand-new building towering over David's town. It was the Herodeum, a combination of fortress and mausoleum, recently erected by King Herod, who was dying inch by inch on his couch of gold.

And now they had reached the end of the journey. The little town of Bethlehem lay before them, terraced on the slope surrounded by vineyards and olive groves. They entered through the city gate. How many, many times during the last days Joseph must have gazed anxiously at his young wife, who each time had smiled bravely back at him. But now all was safe, and his heart was full of thanksgiving. One could imagine that they first wound their way through the crowded streets to the publican's office to fulfill the census which had brought them thither, and then Joseph must have said, "and now, let's go home."

To the Oriental, hospitality is sacred. If there was no room for Joseph in the house of his fathers, it must really have been occupied to the last square yard by relatives who had arrived for the same purpose a little earlier. If one has been in Salzburg during Festival time, or in Oberammergau when the Passion Play is on, and has seen on almost every house the sign "No Room—No Room—No Room," then one can imagine a little bit how it must have been. Joseph pleading from door to door, worming his way through the crowds with his broad shoulders making a way for Mary, who shouldn't be pushed like that. Only after he had tried all the houses of relatives and friends, Joseph decided with a deep sigh to go to the public inn. Bethlehem, unlike Jerusalem, was only a small country place and didn't have one of those larger and more comfortably-equipped tourist homes. There wouldn't be any privacy for Mary. There wouldn't even be cleanliness with all the fresh and rotten manure around the walled-in courtyard. But there was only the choice between the protecting walls of this little inn or the dangers of the open fields, and one more look at Mary showed that she was drooping with fatigue. And then the most crushing of all blows came. There was no room at the inn. Maybe the innkeeper, whose place was overcrowded, didn't even open, but just through the closed door told them harshly to go away. If the onslaught of tourists becomes too great in a small town, the natives often object. If you haven't wired ahead for reservations, well, that's just too bad.

"He came unto his own, and his own received him not" (John 1:11).

Joseph had been chosen by God Almighty to be the guardian of those two most precious lives—the Son of God and His mother. This was now the hour when Joseph showed that he was worthy of his high vocation. In this moment of his keenest disappointment it would have been only human and most understandable if he had lost his nerve a bit and tried once more from house to house, making a big display, imploring, threatening, crying (we are in the Orient!). No, Joseph did not leave Mary's side.

Boys growing up in country towns usually know every square foot of the surroundings for miles. He must have known those limestone caves in which his great ancestor, David, had hidden, and he remembered the one where there was a manger. Once more Joseph took the reins of the donkey and silently led the way towards the only shelter he could provide.

Once when we had come to that point in the Christmas story, Hedwig, who was pretty young then, exclaimed with flashing eyes: "Oh, Mother, if only we had lived in Bethlehem then! We would have taken Mary and Joseph into the big guest room with the balcony." Her little sisters had tears in their eyes, tears of wrath against the bad people, tears of pity for the poor Holy Mother.

Many big and little children must have felt the same way, because there is an age-old folk custom called the "*Herberg Suchen*" (Seeking for Shelter). During the last ten days before Christmas throughout the villages of Austria the people carry an image of the Blessed Mother through the place, leaving it in another house each day, where it is received with great solemnity, being treated as a special guest, given a place of honor, and lovingly decorated with flowers and candles. It is also done in large families, every member taking turns for one day being the special host for the exalted guest.

Our Lord Himself foresaw this reaction of the human heart when He one day would say, "And he that shall receive one such little child in my name, receiveth me" (Matt. 18:5). He does not say: "Whosoever receiveth one of those little ones in My name is doing something very nice and I will bless him for it." He says, "Receiveth Me." Just why don't we take Him literally? If we did, for instance, there couldn't possibly be any little ones left in the big city of New York throughout the hot summer months, playing on the streets in the blue fumes of the exhaust pipes, on the asphalt softened by the heat. The stone-hard asphalt can soften—how about human hearts?

Aren't Mary and Joseph still going from place to place looking for shelter, and isn't it still true that there is no room in the inn? The only change is that this time the innkeepers are we, you and I.

IV

"Silent Night, Holy Night"

I come from Tyrol. This is the part of Austria with the highest mountains and the greatest number of wood carvers. Wood-carving seems to be a talent which is inheritable. There are whole valleys where all the families carve. The favorite objects are the very end and the very beginning of Redemption — the crucifix and the crib. Tyrol is the country of the Christmas Crib. Every home, every church has such a representation of the Nativity, more or less elaborate, more or less artistic. But always the cave is freshly painted and meticulously clean, ox and ass look well-groomed, and the straw may even be a little gilded. When one grows up among those "pretty" cribs, one easily forgets how different it must have been on that first Holy Night. Because there was a manger in the cave, it must have been used for animals, so the floor was littered with dung. Except for that manger, there was nothing in it perhaps but a little barley straw. The only fresh air came through the narrow entrance by which one stepped down into that dark, smelly hole. "To make oneself at home" was quite impossible. Joseph could only try to make Mary a little less uncomfortable by arranging the straw so that she could lean against the wall opposite the entrance, get some fresh air, and look up into the cold winter sky.

The Gospels don't mention the ox and ass, without which every crib would be unthinkable, but Isaias the prophet (1:3) knew of them: "The ox knoweth his owner, and the ass his master's crib." The Gospels also do not mention the cave directly; still, tradition very often supplements the Gospels. After all, didn't St. John the Apostle say

27

that the world itself could not hold the books that would have
to be written if everything should be told in detail? And it is
according to tradition of the very first centuries. St. Justinius
the martyr, living in the generation after the Apostles, and
after him, St. Jerome, living in a cave outside Bethlehem
himself for most of his life, reverently describe this cave of
the Holy Night.

What may have gone on during these next hours of the
most holy of all nights? "And it came to pass," says St. Luke
(2:6-7), "that when they were there, her days were accomplished, that she should be delivered. And she brought
forth her firstborn son, and wrapped him up in swaddling
clothes and laid him in a manger." And tradition adds that
Joseph, who saw that the hour was at hand now for the young
mother and who did not know that she wouldn't need any
aid, went over to Bethlehem to look for a helper among the
women. Mary, however, was drawn in deepest recollection
into God, and when she came out of her ecstasy, there lay
before her her little Child. With what indescribable happiness must she have taken Him, pressed Him to her heart, and
wrapped Him up against the cold. When Joseph returned, he
found mother and Child. Forgotten now was the anxiety of
the last days, the crushing disappointment of the evening,
the coldness of the hearts in Bethlehem, as well as the cold of
the frosty winter night. In this cave there were only love, and
wonder, and adoration. For "The Word was made flesh and
dwelt among us, and we saw his glory" (John 1:14).

V

"Angels We Have Heard on High"

"Christ was born in Bethlehem," but the world didn't notice. The world was asleep. "The light shineth in darkness, and the darkness did not comprehend it." (John 1:5).

Only a few miles away in Jerusalem the house of the Lord God was silent and dark. The priests of the Most High were asleep. Also the king's palace was dark. Herod was seeking relief from his pain in sleep. All the great ones in Israel, the scribes, the doctors of the law, the zealots, the Pharisees, and the Herodians—all were fast asleep. In the little town on the hillside where the family of David the King was gathered together, everybody was fast asleep. All those of the house and family of David had come, some of them from faraway places, to be enrolled as subjects of a foreigner. Now they slept, and didn't know that their Kinsman promised from of old was born in their midst in a cave because there was no room in their homes, in their hearts. In faraway Rome Caesar Augustus was also fast asleep. Little did he know how much his recent law had inconvenienced a humble couple somewhere near the border of the empire. And little would he have cared, had he known. Wouldn't he have been astonished, though, had he learned that throughout the centuries millions and millions would come and go who would never have heard of him, the great Augustus, except in connection with the birth of this humble Child.

All the great ones of this world were asleep, but in heaven was such rejoicing as has never been heard since the creation of the world. All those millions of souls, perhaps headed by Adam and Eve, thanked God in a

thunderous chorus that their Redemption was at hand.
And the Heavenly Father wanted to congratulate His
children on earth—was there no one awake to receive
His messengers?

"I confess to thee, O Father, Lord of heaven and earth,"
Our Lord would pray on a later day, "because thou
hast hid these things from the wise and prudent, and hast revealed them to little ones" (Matt. 11:25). And great St. Paul
would add one day: "But the foolish things of the
world hath God chosen that He may confound the wise:
and the weak things of the world hath God chosen that He
may confound the strong, and the base things of the world,
and the things that are contemptible hath God chosen.
. . ." (I Cor. 1:27-28). The great teachers of the day, the
Rabbis of Israel, had declared the shepherds as "base"
and "foolish," the very lowest of the low, on the same level
as the Gentiles, unclean before the law. And these shepherds were the only ones awake in Israel. "And there
were in the same country shepherds watching and keeping
the night watches over their flock."

This was no ordinary flock they were watching. These
sheep were not to be eaten by men, but they were destined
to become sacrifices for God. At this time the priests of
Jahweh were not only servants of God, but also extremely
successful businessmen. They had managed to become the
sole proprietors of the herds from which the sacrifices were
chosen. Again it is Josephus Flavius who mentions that at
one Easter around 120,000 lambs were slaughtered. That
gives a little idea of the size of the flocks, parts of which
were grazing on the fields outside of Bethlehem. "Behold
the Lamb of God," John the Baptist would exclaim later.
And there the Lamb of God was born next to the lambs of
sacrifice, the fulfillment next to the symbol. But it was the
shepherds, not the owners, who would find out about Him
first. "And behold, an angel of the Lord stood by them,
and the brightness of God shone round about them."

This was not the first time that angels had been sent to
men. Throughout the pages of the Old Testament we find
it happening many times, but each single time when

heaven and earth met, the reaction of earth was the same: "And they feared with a great fear." "We shall certainly die, because we have seen God," cried the father of Samson (Judg. 13:22) because an angel had appeared to him and his wife. How did he know that it was not God Himself? And each time heaven would say to earth: "Fear not, for behold, I bring you good tidings of great joy." Each time except once. Once the great Angel of the Lord was sent on a special mission into a small village tucked away in the hills to a young girl, and this time when the natural and supernatural world met, it was different. The girl did not fall on her face, fearing she must surely die, and the first words of the angel were not "Fear not." Only once did it happen that the Angel of the Lord greeted one of the children of men, and this young girl did not say to the tremendous heavenly guest in the usual bashful way, "Oh no, no sir, not you should greet me, but I have to greet you first." No, she listened to the greeting, and then she only pondered in her heart what it might mean. For in this one case the Angel of the Lord was greeting Mary of Nazareth.

But the shepherds were afraid with the fear of Samson's parents. How must that have been when the brightness of God shone round about them? It is quite good to stop for a moment at such expressions and let our imagination take over. What have we seen in our life which we would call bright? The noonday sun on a summer's day on top of a glacier? The explosion of an atomic bomb? Compared with the "brightness of God," they must be like the flicker of a little candle. And this is what the shepherds saw. And what did the angel himself look like? The shepherds don't tell, but Isaias, hundreds of years before them, had once had a look at the seraphim and described them: "The one had six wings, and the other had six wings. With two they covered his face, and with two they covered his feet, and with two they flew" (Isa. ¾:2).

And who was this angel? We don't know for sure, but tradition has it that it was Gabriel, the Angel of the Incarnation. Now the angel talks; and again let us use our imagination and think of different voices we have heard and which we still remember for their beauty of tone. And again we may be sure that this angelic voice ringing out loud and reassuringly through the night must have been more beautiful than anything we can remember. "Fear not," the angel said, "for, behold, I bring you good tidings of great joy that shall be to all the people. For, this day, is born to you a Saviour who is Christ the Lord in the city of David." It is true that these shepherds were illiterate, and for this they were cursed by the scribes. But this message they did understand, because for this Christ the Lord they had been waiting all their lives that He might come and redeem them from the unbearable burdens which the Pharisees were heaping upon their shoulders, burdens which the Pharisees themselves would not deign to carry.

"And this shall be a sign unto you," continued the angel. "You shall find the infant wrapped in swaddling clothes and laid in a manger." Now the shepherds knew they would not have to go into town and knock from door to door. If He was lying in a manger, it could only be in a certain cave not far away. So the Messiah had come—not as a king on horseback, and not like Melchisedec appearing in great dignity suddenly and mysteriously, but as a little baby wrapped in swaddling clothes, exactly as one of their own children was wrapped up and carried around by their wives.

The very moment when the great angel had finished his message there burst suddenly forth a torrent of heavenly music, and when the shepherds looked up in still more wonder and awe, they saw what the Evangelist would describe as a "multitude of the heavenly army." Daniel of old when he had once had a similar vision, tried to describe it: "A swift stream of fire issued forth from before him: thousand of thousands ministered to him, and ten thousand times a hundred thousand stood before him" (Dan. 7:10). That must be about a "multitude of the heavenly army." And they were now "praising God and saying: Glory to God in the highest, and on earth peace to men of good will." What a choir! And this was the only time the heavenly multitudes are known to have chanted for the children of men. When Isaias had heard them, he said: "And they cried one to another and said: Holy, holy, holy, the Lord God of hosts. All the earth is full of his glory. And the lintels of the doors were moved at the voice of him that cried" (Isa. 6:3-4). Again we might stop for a moment and think of the choirs we have heard in our life: small choirs, large choirs, men's, women's, children's voices; chanting in unison, or singing in parts. And as all human brightness was dimmed when compared with the brightness of God, so all created melody faded before the chant of heaven. There we remember the story told about young Mozart when he came to Rome and listened for the first time to the Sistine Choir performing the *Miserere* composed by Allegri exclusively for the Sistine Chapel. Under threat of excommunication it was forbidden to copy this great work. Mozart, after having listened to it once, returned to his hotel room and wrote it down from memory. What a pity that none of the shepherds handed on the song of the first Gloria!

And what happened then? When the angels left the shepherds, there was no argument, no round-table discussion with which we people of the twentieth century so often kill the sound of the heavenly message in our hearts. They simply "said to one another, Let us go over to Bethlehem and let us see this word that is come to pass, which the Lord hath shewed to us. And they came with haste and they found Mary and Joseph and the infant lying in the manger. And seeing, they understood of the word that had been spoken to them concerning this child."

We don't have to say, "Oh, I wish I had been there." It is not over yet. Christ the Lord is still being born to us, if we just learn to see Him lying helpless and in poverty. Then it could be said of us also what we can say of those shepherds: "You shepherds—'blessed are the eyes that see the things which you see. . . . Many prophets and kings have desired to see the things that you see, and have not seen them; and to hear the things that you hear, and have not heard them'" (Luke 10:23-24).

VI

Mary pondered in her heart

There is a certain flavor to the days after a child is born into a home. Gratefulness that all went well, a deep relief from anxiety, a new happiness and a more tender love hover over the household. All this must have been true of the very first Christian family who ever lived, only much more so. Of the young girl mother it is told that she didn't need any help, neither for herself nor for her little Child. She was able to take care of Him alone right away. "And she brought forth her firstborn son, and wrapped him up in swaddling clothes and laid him in a manger" (Luke 2:7).

We can imagine Joseph going into Bethlehem every day, partly to buy fresh food, and partly to watch how the census was going. In forty days he would have to present mother and Child in the temple, and from what they had just gone through on their winter's journey, they decided to wait in Bethlehem. Of course, Joseph was trying to get his family out of the cave, and so he kept looking for a house. At the same time he may have been looking for a job. When he came back from his trips into town, he told Mary that the shepherds couldn't get over the things they had heard and seen on that unforgettable night, and had told their friends and neighbors. "And all that heard wondered: and at those things that were told them by the shepherds" (Luke 2:18). What did Mary do about this? She "kept all these words, pondering them in her heart" (Luke 2:19).

The way people react to important happenings in their lives, may they be exceedingly happy or sad, gives the deepest insight into their character. Just let's look around us. What is the usual reaction among our friends and neighbors if in a family something unexpected happens? Let us say the father of the family suddenly loses his whole fortune, or he is unexpectedly promoted to a big job. What is the usual reaction? Telephone and telegraph are immediately put to work, letters are written by the score, and the incident is discussed for days on end. It is no wonder that there is no time left in which to ponder on what it might mean, what message God might want to bring home to us by permitting this or that to happen in our lives.

"To ponder" is just another word for "to meditate on" or simply "to think about." With a special effort some of us might set aside fifteen minutes a day out of a sense of duty to ponder upon divine things. This time of meditation can turn into a real bother, and we may spend it looking at the watch. At the slightest provocation we gladly omit it. We are very easily "too busy to keep it up," but with Mary it seems to be second nature. Already as a child in the temple she must have been meditating on the law of the Lord all the days of her life, as it says in Psalm 118. The splendor of the House of God, the starry sky at night, the countryside of Judea, the Word of God as it was read to her from ancient scrolls by her teachers — everything was one big meditation book for her telling of the grandeur, and also of the mercy of God. She never grew tired of pondering on all those things in her heart.

If we would only give it a try and introduce this attitude into our homes, families and schools again, teach our children to think things over in their hearts! The Quakers do it—why not all of us? This is an all-but-forgotten art in our days. Who thinks? We don't need to any more. The T.V. and Radio do it for us, and the daily papers, magazines, digests, and quite recently, digests of digests. Once when we attended a symphony concert at the Academy of Music in Philadelphia, a lady from the Main Line tapped me on the shoulder and said: "Baroness, I would be very much obliged if you could tell me what I should think about this concert." It sounds funny, but one should not laugh, one should cry at such poverty. How

different it was with Mary, who started a life of pondering
early in her youth!

There must have been visitors in the cave in that first
week, only simple people because the highbrows didn't
have anything to do with such castaways as the shepherds.
Visiting in the Orient is identical with bringing gifts, and
the shepherds give milk, butter, cheese, and bread, as the
carols tell us.

While Mary and Joseph were tending to the simple
chores of those days, cleaning out the cave, tending to the
Child, tending to the animals, receiving the shepherds
with their families and friends, the king of Israel in his
palace, thousands of God's priests, and all those scribes
and Pharisees only a few miles away didn't know what the
smallest shepherd child in the valley of Bethlehem knew.
This is the secret of God, Who can only be found and recognized by simple hearts.

Toward the end of this week Joseph had to make preparations for the Circumcision. This was a ceremony of the
pious Jews which goes back to Abram. He was once called
out of his tent at night and God told him: "Look up to
heaven and number the stars, if thou canst. And He said
to him: So shall thy seed be" (Gen. 15:5). There the first
covenant, "The Old Testament" was contracted between
God and men. At this time Abram was given a new name,
Abraham. This is the origin of the custom that a Jewish
child is given his name at his Circumcision.

On the evening before that day, it was customary
throughout the country for the parents of the baby to invite the children of the neighborhood for a party. The
new baby was shown to them. So Joseph went out to invite
the children of the shepherds, and when they came, Mary
and Joseph entertained their little guests and showed
them their new-born Baby. And they still do so year after
year, Christmas Week having become a big children's
party all over the world.

The Circumcision was performed by the Jewish priests
or elders in the homes of the people, not in the temple or
synagogue. We know from St. Luke that when little St.

John was circumcised, there was a great feast with all the friends and neighbors present. Such family feasts are always accompanied in the Orient by a meal, and there is always a crowd of poor people gathered at such events, sure of some alms.

On the eighth day Joseph went to Bethlehem and returned with a priest and a woman who assisted at such occasions. They brought the Circumcision Stool and a slab of stone around two feet in diameter, the Circumcision Stone, and there was a knife and a few boxes with ointments. A small carpet was spread on the rough floor of the cave, and everything was set up. The priest took the Child out of the arms of the mother. They prayed and sang for some time, and then the priest asked the father which name the Child should be given. "Jesus," said Joseph, as it had been announced by the angel. The woman showed the troubled young mother how to attend to the wound, then they wrapped the Child tightly in red and white swaddling clothes, and the ceremony was over. With the gifts of the shepherds, they arranged now a little meal, and the rest they gave to the poor. The Child was crying and restless, and Mary and Joseph tried to soothe Him by carrying Him up and down the cave.

Suffering had entered into this little family. Suffering calls forth compassion; compassion, however, deepens love. This is the way it works in every ordinary family, and this is exactly the way it happened in the Holy Family. Oh, we can't start soon enough to get these holiest three persons out of the picture frames, down from the niches, and let them become again what they really were — breathing, warm-blooded people with hearts full of emotions. There was in the cave on that day a father, a mother, and a suffering little Child. What may they have said and done to each other, and what may they have said and done to the little Baby? I can't forget how one of my children once said: "In the Holy Family they never laughed or cried, did they?"

"They most certainly did," I answered with emphasis. "Why not?"

"But weren't they too holy?" Asked the little one with awe.

It is all so wrong; and the statues in the churches, and the holy cards in the books have a great deal to do with it. But let us get down to facts. When God in His eternal wisdom resolved to redeem mankind, He had infinite ways in which to do it. There were shapes and forms we can think of, such as sending the Messiah as an angel in great power and glory, or as a mighty king on horseback, then there are many more possibilities which we in our limited mind can't even conceive. But no, Almighty God chose none of those ways, but instead, sent His only Son as a little Child into a family. Men have founded orders, congregations, and organizations; God's own foundation is the Christian family. A real mother, a real father, and a real Child, living, loving, suffering — not symbols, but people like us. If this was God's own and only choice from those myriad, infinite possibilities, then we should say, "Amen, so be it." That means in this case that instead of having a "devotion to the Holy Family," we must treat the Holy Family in a way as our next-door neighbors, become acquainted with them, go visiting, invite them over, watch them all the while, and ponder about them in our hearts. "For God so loved the world that He gave His only begotten Son, that whosoever believes in Him will not perish, but have everlasting life" (John 3:16). Only then does it make sense that God became man and cried as a little Baby in His mother's arms. If we do this, we shall very soon find how we keep pondering in our hearts, because there will be so very much to ponder about that one short life won't be time enough. It will take eternity.

VII

candlemas day

There are many things we really don't know about the childhood story of Our Lord and there is absolutely no way of
finding out. For instance, how long the census may have
taken in Bethlehem, how long the little town was overcrowded and how soon Joseph could take his family from the
cave into a house. In a way, it doesn't matter and in a way it
does. As soon as you have started to re-live the life of Our
Lord together with your family as closely as possible day by
day—you discover that this is something which has a beginning but no end. The more one has found out, the more one
still has to find out. As soon as the children's interest is
aroused, questions will never cease. This is a typical one:
How long was the Holy Family in the cave? Once in a while it
will happen that even after much research you will have to
say, "I really don't know"; but this is already great progress
compared with those who, when asked this same question,
answer, "What do I care?"

Our children wanted to have a day by day account. Now
the priest of the Circumcision has left with the woman and
the implements. What happened next? We figured out together that the next days and nights might have been pretty
unquiet with a sick Baby in the house. When the wound had
healed and little Jesus smiled again, how relieved Mary and
Joseph must have felt.

"And how about the census?" said one of the youngsters.
"Didn't Joseph have to go downtown and announce the
new name?"

This was a good question. Surely Joseph had to do that,
and so we accompanied him "downtown" to Bethlehem,

as he approached once more the census taker, and watched how for the first time in history the Holy Name was written down. This was not an uncommon name, and in the way of His days it was spelled Joshua or Jeshua.

Even if we don't know how long, we may be sure it was as soon as possible that Joseph got his little family into a house in Bethlehem. The next thing was to find out how the house in Bethlehem looked. With the help of pictures from illustrated articles and postal cards sent by friends from their pilgrimages of the Holy Land, we easily found out what the houses looked like.

What I am telling here does not refer to the happenings of one year. It also is not story-telling to children. It is honest-to-goodness research work done by a whole family throughout the years. Your interest, once aroused, will compel you to watch our for illustrated articles about the Holy Land and to keep postal cards from there. A map of the Holy Land will soon prove to be an absolute must. What fun it was when we also found a map of Vermont on the same scale and put the two on the wall next to each other to compare. From Nazareth to Bethlehem it was about as far as from Stowe to Rutland, or a little less. From Jerusalem to Bethlehem it would be five miles south of Stowe and one mile east. It is a good idea to take a family hike of just this distance once, both ways on foot, of course, because soon we accompany the Holy Family on their way to Jerusalem, to the temple.

"And after the days of her purification according to the law of Moses were accomplished, they carried him to Jerusalem to present him to the Lord."

"The days of her purification—" refers to a law in the Old Testament. "She shall touch no holy thing," it says of a mother after she has given birth to a child, "neither shall she enter into the sanctuary, until the days of her purification be fulfilled" (Lev. 12:4). This was forty days if the child was a boy, and eighty days if the child was a girl, that the mother could not enter the temple and was liturgically unclean. Then the law continues: "And when the days of her purification are expired, for a son, or for a daughter, she shall bring to the door of the tabernacle of the testimony, a lamb of a year old for a holocaust, and a young pigeon or a turtle for sin, and shall deliver them to the priest, who shall offer them before the Lord, and shall pray for her: and so shall be cleansed. . . . And if her hand find not sufficiency, and she is not able to offer a lamb, she shall take two turtles, or two young pigeons, one for a holocaust, and another for sin: and the priest shall pray for her, and so she shall be cleansed'' (Lev. 12:6-8). Right away the idea comes to one's mind: Mary was not allowed to touch any holy thing—but there she was carrying holiness itself around in her arms, and she was not supposed to enter into the sanctuary of the temple.

After the purification of the mother there was still another law to fulfill, and that was the presentation of the boy: ''And the Lord spoke to Moses, saying: Sanctify unto me every firstborn that openeth the womb among the children of Israel, as well of men as of beasts: for they are all mine'' (Exod. 13:1-2).

This law served as a reminder to the Jews that God had once slain the Egyptians and taken their firstborn sons but had spared the firstborn of the Hebrews. Now in order that the child might go back home with his parents and not have to remain in the temple for the service of the Lord, the parents had to pay a certain sum in silver—about five dollars in our money—as ransom money. This was the law for eleven of the twelve tribes of Israel. The sons of the tribe of Aaron, however, were destined to the priesthood. No money had to be paid for them. So Jesus' little cousin John, belonging to the tribe of Aaron, did not fall under that law. Jesus, belonging to the tribe of Juda, did.

One of the great beauties of reading through the Gospels like this is that after doing it a while, it will very often happen that the passage you are reading will bring to mind another one. Young minds are especially keen at finding such apropos comparisons. Therefore, having worked on ''the days of her purification,'' one of the family might muse: ''But Mary had been greeted by the angel, 'Hail, full of grace.' Didn't she know that the birth of this Child couldn't possibly make her liturgically unclean? And then —the same angel had said to her, He . . . shall be called the Son of the Most High and the Lord God shall give unto him the throne of David his father . . . and of his Kingdom there shall be no end.' Didn't she feel within herself that this Son would not have to be bought with ransom money?''

And the family circle decides that she must have known. But in her actions she now accepted what this her Son would later express in words to His cousin the Baptist when he didn't want to baptize Him, but would rather have been baptized by Him: "Suffer it to be so now. For so it becometh us to fulfill all justice" (Matt. 3:15).

A few years ago we were talking about this same subject, and again we came to the point that Our Lord really didn't *have* to follow the law, when young Rosmarie remarked: "Well, isn't this exactly like the story with the income tax?"

(It was February, on the Feast of the Presentation, and the phrase "income tax" must have been heard frequently around the house.)

"Which story with the income tax?" We asked, somewhat dumfounded.

"Oh," said Rosmarie, "wasn't Our Lord once reminded that He hadn't paid His tax yet, and didn't He say to Peter, His friend, pretty clearly that He didn't have to?" Feverishly turning the pages in her New Testament, she had found the place (Matt. 17:24-26) and read it to us triumphantly.

" 'What is thy opinion, Simon? The kings of the earth, of whom do they receive tribute or custom? Of their own children, or of strangers?' "

In her own words she continued, "And Peter would say, 'Of strangers, of course.' " Then returning to the Book: " 'Then the children are free. But that we may not scandalize them, go to the sea and cast in a hook: and that fish which shall first come up, take: and when thou hast opened its mouth, thou shalt find a stater: take that and give it to them for me and thee.' "

It is a real feast if oneself or someone in the family finds such connections as the "story if the income tax." So it is pretty safe to say: Of course, Mary knew, but "that we may not scandalize them," she prepared for the three-fold ceremonies: her purification, the presentation of the Son, and the sacrifice for sin.

Pitilessly the children want to know: "What happened in those weeks before they went to the temple?"

The Gospel doesn't say. No contemporary of those days is still living, no photographs were taken, no diaries were kept. But it must have happened *somehow*, and in all reverence, my guess is as good as yours. For instance, Ain Karim, the home of Zachary and Elizabeth, was only about a mile and a half away from Bethlehem in the hill country. Isn't it more than likely that within these forty days of waiting Elizabeth would show up and repay the visit of her young cousin? Most probably she would bring Zachary and her baby boy. How much rejoicing there would be among the two families. With what happiness would the Magnificat be recited again, and the Benedictus!

We don't know anything about the parents of Mary, but tradition has it that their names were Joachim and Anna. The Church celebrates their feasts in July. Down to the earliest times of Christianity, the artists used to picture St. Anne as a happy grandmother with her daughter, Mary and her little Grandson. Couldn't it be that some people from Nazareth returning from the census in Bethlehem brought the message to Anne that the Baby had arrived, and her daughter and son-in-law would wait those forty days near Jerusalem? What would any mother in our days think and do in such a case? She would exclaim: "Oh, my poor girl! She only took the most necessary things for emergency with her. I must get her everything she could possibly need." And then the elderly woman might start out on the trip herself, impatient to see the precious Grandchild.

Sure, this is all "might be" and "maybe," but if I want to bring those forty days of waiting to life, I certainly must use all my God-given faculties: the intellect and the memory, for studying, and finally the other one just as God-given, imagination, to be applied lovingly to reading between the lines. If we only consider what a part imagination plays in public life, in the world of fiction writing, moving pictures, radio and television! It couldn't possibly be put to better use than to help us to perceive how He did what He did, or what He looked like when He said certain things. It seems as if only the painters have made use of this privilege "to figure it all out." When we think of the "Annunciations," the "Visitations," and the "Nativities" as they were imagined by painters and sculptors throughout the centuries, it should serve as a stimulus to our imagination. "All right, that's the way Giotto or Raphael, Michelangelo or Albrecht Dürer saw it. Which way would you and I picture it?" And isn't it a shame that you and I would most probably have to admit that we "hadn't gotten around yet to thinking about it," and just took Raphael and Fra Angelico and their pitiful descendants from Barclay Street and St. Sulpice as substitutes.

It is said that in the fourth century the market women in Constantinople were throwing cabbage heads at each other because they had different opinions about the Most Holy Trinity. Isn't it rather sad that we have to admit that while market women might still throw cabbage heads at each other, the reasons for doing so have changed so completely. Who cares now, for instance, what happened to Jesus, Mary, and Joseph while they were waiting for the days of her purification to be fulfilled?

Finally the morning of the great feast day dawned. Mary and Joseph must have set out with the Child very early that morning to be in time for the morning sacrifice in the temple, after which the mothers used to be purified.

Joseph on their journey down had probably told Mary all about his home town and introduced her to Bethlehem —now it was Mary's turn. They were nearing her second home now — the temple. Tradition tells us that Mary had been brought to the House of God when she was three years old. Every year we celebrate the feast of her presentation in November. As a temple virgin she spent her whole youth within the holy walls of the cloister together with other young girls from the first families. It was the highest education a young woman in Israel could get. They were taught how to read and write. If we consider that all boys had to learn to read (only the boys, not the girls), but not how to write, we understand what a privilege it was to be a temple virgin. They were instructed in Holy Scriptures, some of which, like the Psalms and the Proverbs, they had to learn by heart. They were taught how to cook and took turns cooking for the priests. They learned how to spin and weave and embroider. Is it any wonder that they were the most sought-after brides in Israel? The temple, besides being the House of the Most High, was for Mary also her home, her Alma Mater; the fondest memories of her youth were connected with it. Only a year or two had she been away from this sacred place, but how much had happened to her in that short time. First her espousal to Joseph, then the earthshaking moment of the Annunciation; her visit with Elizabeth, maybe the happiest months of her life; then the heartrendering weeks when she witnessed Joseph's worries; the trip down to Bethlehem; the mystery of the Holy Night; the shepherds and their story about the angels—and how here she came back to the temple not alone, but with her husband and her Son, pondering in her heart the great things said to her by the angel and by Elizabeth.

The temple! How much do we know about it, its shape, its size, its services, its porches, gates and courts, its priests? For Our Lord it will always be the House of the Father. It will be said of Him in the words of the Sixty-eighth Psalm: "The zeal of thy house hath eaten me up" (John 2:17). One day He will cleanse it in vigor and wrath. Of the last days of His life it is said: "And he was teaching daily in the temple" (Luke 19:47). Just how familiar are we with it? Most of us do not give it a second thought and take the temple simply for something like a big church. How astonished are we, therefore, when we find out that at that time the temple occupied a square of more than 950 feet. This would make it more than half again as long as St. Peter's in Rome, which measures 613 feet. During recent excavations of the temple stones have been found measuring from twenty to forty feet in length and weighing about one hundred tons. In the back of the large Confraternity edition of the New Testament is a colored plan which gives us an idea. Soon we find ourselves hunting for pictures and more information and, if possible, a scale model. They are very rarely to be found, though, so why not make one yourself? It is exciting and interesting. There are whole books written on the temple, one by Alfred Edersheim: *The Temple, Its Ministry and Services as They Were in the Time of Christ;* and in a book by Father O'Shea, *Mary and Joseph, Their Life and Times,* are three very helpful chapters on the temple: "The Priests of Jehovah," "The House of Jehovah," and "The Hour of Incense." If, after some study, we try to reconstruct the temple on a small scale with our girls and boys—must not Our Lord be pleased that we show so much interest in the House of the Father so dear to His Heart? After having worked with cardboard, paper and glue for weeks that way, we shall find ourselves richly rewarded, because we don't feel like strangers any more, but understand better when we read together in the New Testament: "Then the devil took him up into the holy city and set him upon the pinnacle of the temple" (Matt. 4:5); "Zacharias the son of Barachias, whom you killed between the temple and the altar" (Matt. 23:35); "And casting down the pieces of silver in the temple" (Matt. 27:5). "And when he was walking in the temple" (Mark 11:27); "Two men went up into the temple to pray" (Luke 18:10); "I was daily with you in the temple teaching" (Mark 14:49); "Jesus therefore cried out in the temple" (John 7:28); "And behold the veil of the temple was rent in two from the top even to the bottom" (Matt. 27:51); "Begging alms at the Beautiful gate of the temple" (Acts 3:10).

How closely can we accompany the Holy Family when they pass through the royal gate entering the temple. First they walked through the royal cloisters, a hall bigger than any Christian basilica has ever been, a richly carved roof carried by 162 beautiful pillars a hundred feet high. There were benches for everyone who wanted to rest. This was the place for all the beggars and the blind and deaf and dumb and those afflicted with many a sickness, all of them exhibiting their troubles to move the charity of the many passers-by. At that time there were no hospitals in Jerusalem, and no Board of Social Welfare. After they had passed the covered cloister, the Holy Family stepped out into the vast Court of the Gentiles. Here were the tables of the money changers and the temple markets. As pilgrims came to Jerusalem from every nation under heaven, they were forced to change their foreign currency into the temple coins. And a long story could be told about the temple markets and all the crooked business going on there. That's where Mary and Joseph bought the two turtle doves because they were so poor they could not afford to buy a lamb. Mary carried her Child, and Joseph the turtle doves and the money. They went across the vast open court up to the barrier, a wall about four feet high bearing inscriptions in Greek telling the Gentiles to go no farther under penalty of death. But Mary and Joseph were allowed by the guards to pass. The real temple buildings were rising before them now. Up a flight of fifteen steps they came to the gate called "Beautiful," eighty feet high and thirty feet wide, made of heavy Corinthian bronze. The Holy Family approached the Court of the Women. There were many halls and latticed galleries. Crossing through, they came to another splendid gate called Nicanor. Outside this gate, which was made of silver and gold, they had to wait until they heard the silver trumpets blow. This was the sign of the closing of the morning sacrifice. Now the mothers to be purified lined up on the steps. "And Mary the Mother of Jesus was there, too." Through the golden bars she could see the huge altar from which clouds of incense rose, and behind it, the tremendous façade of the House of God. If Mary looked, she could see through the open door the magnificent veil. Perhaps her own hands helped to weave it. The other women standing there with Mary on that morning must have gazed with awe at the veil behind which was the Holy of Holies. Nobody paid any special attention to the most beautiful of the mothers waiting there, not the other women, not the fifty priests around the altar, not the guards of the temple police. Nobody knew that the God of Israel had really come to His house this morning—in the arms of the beautiful maiden.

Now the deep tones of the great organ called the Magraphah were to be heard. The white-robed priests came to accept the doves for the sin offering. The birds were taken in, killed, some of the blood spilling on the altar, and their flesh had to be eaten by the priests on the grounds of the temple. Some of the birds were burned, and the ceremony of the purification was over. All the mothers had become liturgically clean again. After this came the ceremony of the presentation. Out of the group of women, only the mothers with firstborn sons approached the priest, presenting the baby to him. Two blessings were spoken: one in thanksgiving for the birth of a son, and the other had to do with the law of ransom. The five shekels were handed over to the priest, and the ceremony was finished. It was finished for all the mothers except one. When Mary went down the steps to meet Joseph and they both were just about to disappear humbly in the great stream of worshipers, they were stopped by a venerable old man. It was Simeon, of whom it is said that: "This man was just and devout, waiting for the consolation of Israel. And the Holy Ghost was in him" (Luke 2:25). By the inspiration of the Spirit he came into the temple. He had been waiting at the foot of the steps watching the women coming down, all young mothers proud and happy. When he saw the most beautiful, the most radiant of them all, the Holy Ghost revealed to him that the beautiful little Child in her arms was the son of God. This was the most sublime moment of his long life. He approached her and stretched his arms out. Looking into the old face, she handed the Child to him. What emotions must have filled the heart of the old man when he pressed his infant Saviour to his heart, breaking out into the canticle of joy, "Nunc dimittis. . . . " "And his father and mother were wondering at those things which were spoken concerning him. And Simeon blessed them and said to Mary his mother: Behold this child is set for the fall and for the resurrection of many in Israel and for a sign which shall be contradicted. And thy own soul a sword shall pierce, that out of many hearts, thoughts may be revealed'' (Luke 2:33-35). He handed back the Child to His mother, who received Him in deep silence, pondering over this terrible prophecy.

Then before they could turn around to go home, there came an old lady, a widow of eighty-four years. She must have been in the temple during Mary's time, because it says of her that she "departed not from the temple, by fastings and prayers serving night and day" (Luke 2:37). Old Anna had also been told the secret by the Holy Ghost. That's why she came up that very hour and began to give praise to the Lord. Then she turned around and "spoke of him to all that looked for the redemption of Israel" (Luke 2:38). One can't help asking: "And who were those? Obviously they were none of the great ones in the temple, the mighty and powerful ones, because nothing at all happened. The Holy Family quietly left the House of God.

What must have been going on in Mary's heart? She knew that she was the mother of the Messiah. As a temple virgin she had learned all the Messianic prophecies by heart, and from the Twenty-first Psalm she knew the horrible fate that awaited the One Who would redeem His people. But maybe she hoped that the Heavenly Father might change His mind, as He had done with Nineveh when He had sent the Prophet Jonas into the town with the strict message that Nineveh was to be destroyed. Then when He saw the repentance and good will of the people, He forgave and Nineveh was not destroyed. Well, if Mary had ever had such hopes for the future of her Son, Simeon had destroyed them; and while they were walking back to their humble home in Bethlehem in deep silence meditating on what had happened, the sword of which he had spoken had already begun to pierce her soul.

"Mother, and what does that mean, 'That, out of many

hearts, thoughts may be revealed'?'' asks one of the children. Yes — what does that mean?

Years have passed since that question was asked. At least once a year we meditate on this part of the Gospels, and we are still pondering this question in our hearts.

VIII

Caspar, Melchior, and Balthasar

It was a few years ago, and a wonderful winter day. I had been working with Hester, my secretary, in my little house which is halfway up the hill behind the big house, and after a quick supper in the main house, had returned there to work. We had just admired one of our gorgeous mountain sunsets and were about to light the kerosene lamp when I saw something coming up the slope. It looked as if a big yellow star were climbing up the hill. Hester and I went out onto the porch, and now we saw that we had visitors. In the deep snow, those colorful but quaintly dressed figures looked very much like foreigners. The first one was on horseback, and the star kept right above him, while the other two had a hard time wading through the knee-deep snow. One of them swung a censer, and the sweet fragrance of incense filled the crisp winter air. Finally they all arrived, and lining up, enveloped in pungent clouds, they sang:

> "We three Kings of Orient are,
> Bearing gifts we traverse afar
> Field and fountain, moor and mountain,
> Following yonder star.
> Oh-h—Star of wonder, star of light. . . ."

At this moment Peanuts, the pony, had to sneeze. He wasn't used to incense. While the Holy Kings were singing beautifully and clearly in three parts, I recognized my two best brocade aprons acting as Turkish trousers on the legs dangling from Peanuts. I had a pretty good suspicion that they belonged to little Johannes, but was not quite sure yet because his countenance was dark black, and so was the little fist holding the stick with the star, a masterpiece consisting of transparent paper, cardboard, a flashlight battery and bulb, and the longest broomstick in the house. The other two royalties were dressed in the best silk curtains from the living and dining rooms, and wore the most beautiful golden crowns on their heads. His black majesty was wearing a white turban under his crown, a very becoming contrast to his complexion.

I knew now without looking at the calendar that it must be January 5. These were the "Star Singers" *(Sternsaenger)*, an old Austrian custom going back through the centuries. On the evening of the Epiphany the children dress up as the three Holy Kings and go from house to house singing. There is only one great difference between the original Holy Kings and their little imitators: The first ones brought gifts, the others expect them. They get apples and oranges, dried figs and prunes, cookies and candies, and sometimes also a little money. I felt very much embarrassed at being caught unawares and asked Hester in a whisper whether we had anything in that line in our little study. We didn't, so I quickly invented paper money of my own, worth fifty cents each, which could be cashed in Father Wasner's room. The grateful little Kings—Ili, Lorli, and Johannes, our three youngest ones—sang a thank-you song, through which Peanuts impatiently and understandably pawed the ground. According to the color of his King, he must have come from Africa and not be used to our Vermont winters. Then in majesty and dignity they descended the hill "following yonder star."

Meanwhile the real stars had come out, and the thin sickle of the new moon was hanging in the ink-blue sky over Stowe Hollow. Traces of incense were still around us, and it had all been so poetic and a little unreal that Hester and I stood and watched until the big yellow star had disappeared among the old apple trees and the young voices were trailing off. Only now did we notice how cold it was, and went back in to our little wood stove. The kerosene lamp, however, was not lit that whole evening.

Hester, who had not known this folk custom, found it very lovely and said musingly: "How much does one really know about the story of the three Holy Kings?"

Well, this has been foremost among our research projects for many a Christmas, so I told her what we had discovered. "When Jesus therefore was born in Bethlehem of Judea, in the days of King Herod," so says the second chapter of the Gospel of St. Matthew, "behold, there came wise men from the east to Jerusalem, saying, Where is he that is born king of the Jews? For we have seen his star in the east, and are coming to adore him."

Who were those wise men from the East? Since the third century, going back to Tertullian, there is a tradition which calls them "Magi" and "Kings." This fits perfectly with the Seventy-first Psalm where it says: "The kings of Tharsis and the islands shall offer presents: the kings of the Arabians and of Saba shall bring gifts." Among the old Medes and Persians such Magi were known, a very exclusive caste who led strict lives and kept the fire going at their places of worship in the mountains and studied the stars of heaven and the dreams of men. These men must have heard of the prophecy: "A star shall rise out of Jacob and a sceptre shall spring up from Israel" (Num. 24:17). The Jews, who had been led into captivity several times, had spread the knowledge of a coming Messiah all over the Orient and deep into Persia, where the adventure of Tobias and Esther had taken place. The only thing the Gospel of St. Matthew tells us about the three high personages is that they were wise men and came from the Orient. Now also from the Orient come many legends and stories. One such story says that the Magi were descendants of the great Balaam. The golden coins they brought to little Jesus had been coined by Tarah, the father of Abraham, and Joseph, the son of Jacob, had given them to the people in Sheba when he bought the fragrant spices for the embalming of his father Jacob. It is interesting that the Gospel doesn't talk about the number, how many there were, but in all pictures and pieces of sculpture there are always three.

Some people say they represent the three ages of men: youth, maturity, and old age. Others say they are the representatives of different races: the Semitic, the Caucasian, and the Negro. People gave them the names of Caspar, Melchior, and Balthasar. An old Christian tradition says that St. Thomas baptized them on his way to India, and now their relics are venerated in the Cathedral of Cologne.

How much can one find out about the star? There are many hypotheses. One says it must have been a comet, another says it was a newly appearing star, again another one thinks it was not a star at all, but a strong light like the lights of the Zodiac, which are frequently visible in the Orient. These and many other theories of a more learned nature have been used to explain the words: "We have seen his star in the east."

The Church has not decided on any one of these details, so we in our family have settled on this story. We are all descended from Noah and his family: "And the sons of Noe who came out of the ark, were Shem, Ham, and Japheth . . . and from these was all mankind spread over the whole earth" (Gen. 9:18-19). The white race, or Caucasian race, descended from Japheth; the Mongolian, with all the red and yellow people, from Shem; and the Ethiopian, or black race, from Ham. The story which we like best is this: In Ethiopia, in Persia, and far away in the Caucasus, wise men were watching the sky for a special star which was promised to mankind. On one and the same day they all saw it appear and decided independently of each other, not even knowing of each other, to go and adore the newborn King whose sign the star had been. It took them many months to prepare a caravan worthy of royalty. When their plan became known, they were warned against their undertaking and finally ridiculed. After starting on their way, it took them many more months, and finally one blessed day they were brought *together* by the star in the desert. Now they traveled the last stretch of their journey *together* until at last they saw the high mountains of Moab appearing on the horizon. These were the mountains which Balaam, the great ancestor of all Magi, climbed up with the intention of cursing the people of Israel, and instead he blessed them. These are the mountains on whose peak Moses had stood in silence gazing into the Promised Land which he was not allowed to enter. From these mountains of Moab, the Magi looked down into this canyon which is the Jordan Valley. Now they knew they were near the end of their journey. How much time had they spent on the road? We don't know, but each one had come a tremendous distance, and the caravans of old made about ten or twelve miles a day. When they approached the Jordan, their animals must have drunk greedily after having crossed the desert. They came into Jericho, which had been just newly rebuilt by King Herod. There were the boundaries of the Roman Empire, and customs officers must have searched their rich caravans. Now they were really on the way to Jerusalem. It was that feared stretch of wild countryside infested with robbers, but a strong party such as theirs did not have to worry. Soon they were in the hills of Judea, and finally they saw the walls of the Holy City and the temple of stone and gold rising above it.

They entered through the city gate and asked the first person they met: "Where is he that is born King of the Jews? For we have seen his star in the east and are come to adore him." This question was overheard by the Gestapo.

"By whom?" asked Hester who had been listening in rapt attention, but who couldn't fit this modern word into our ancient Oriental story. The spell was broken, and now we could just as well feed our little stove before it grew cold.

"St. Matthew continues," I said to Hester: " 'And King Herod hearing this was troubled, and all Jerusalem with him' " (Matt. 2:3).

From all I have read and learned about King Herod, he reminds me very much of Hitler and, coming from an invaded country where one had to beware of the Gestapo who, as the saying went, "heard the grass grow," I understand how all Jerusalem was troubled. This Herod had not a drop of Jewish blood in his veins. His father was a Bedouin from Idumea, and his mother an Arabian princess. Of course, he was no descendant of David. He had gotten to the throne by kowtowing to the Romans. When they finally made him king of the Jews, they little knew that they were fulfilling the prophecy: "The sceptre shall not be taken away from Judah . . . till he come that is to be sent: and he shall be the expectation of nations" (Gen. 49:10). In order to make it look a little better, he married Mariamne, the granddaughter of the last real priest king Hyrcanus. Her family was very little pleased about this, and so he simply began to liquidate them. He killed old Hyrcanus and Alexandra his daughter, Mariamne's mother. Mariamne herself was the only being he ever really loved in his life, but one day in a fit of jealousy, he killed her with his own hands. Then he drowned his brother-in-law, the young high priest Aristobulos because he got too popular for Herod's taste. Soon afterwards his own two sons had to be strangled in the bath. When Herod was already very sick, he had his third son beheaded. No wonder his subjects hated him! By and by he had built up such an efficient system of secret police that whatever happened in Jerusalem he knew of within five minutes. Exactly like the Gestapo. Therefore, when those harmless strangers asked for the newborn King, we can understand how all of Jerusalem was troubled because this was the feared word Herod could not stand. During the time of his reign there had been much bloodshed, mass massacre as well as single murders. A rumor had swept through the city that Herod, who was by now dying, had arranged in his last will that immediately upon his death a mass murder was to take place and all the leading men in the nation were to be killed, in order that "there might be tears shed in the Jewish nation on the day of his death."

"You see, Hester," I said, "it must have been pretty similar in the little country of the Jews to our own small Austria. Both had been invaded, and were ruled by Quislings, and both had a Gestapo, the fear of which takes a long, long time to get out of your bones. Therefore, I can so very well understand that the Evangelist said: 'King Herod hearing this was troubled, and all Jerusalem with him.' "

Who is going to be killed next? was the question everyone turned over in his mind. Then the Gospel continues: "And assembling together all the chief priests and the scribes of the people, he inquired of them where Christ should be born" (Matt. 2:4).

In an incredibly short time, the news must have reached Herod that this big, rich caravan with those very strange-looking foreigners had entered Jerusalem. Immediately he summoned the Sanhedrin, and the seventy-two members would obey the royal call immediately because it is not safe to delay when a Hitler calls. Everyone in the city must have held his breath, and the seventy-two dignified elders must have wondered if they were going to leave the palace alive.

When they were admitted into the presence of the king, they salaamed until their beards touched the ground. When they were finished with the ceremonial bows and glanced at the face of their king, the Jews could read there that Herod was troubled. When he glared at them in contempt—that is all he ever had for his Jewish subjects, he the great admirer of the Greeks—there must have been an almost unbearable tension in the room: What does he want of us? What is he going to do now?

When he finally snapped the question: "Where is the Christ to be born?" with an almost unbelieving sigh of relief they broke out with the answer—not only a spokesman, but "they" said to him, says the Gospel: "In Bethlehem of Judea, for so it is written by the prophet." And then they quoted the age-old prophecy of Micah as of one voice: "And thou Bethlehem the land of Judah art not the least among the princes of Judah: for out of thee shall come forth the captain that shall rule my people Israel" (Mic. 5:2).

That was all. He didn't want to hear any more. They were dismissed. It must have been almost too good to be true for them. And now the dying tyrant was thinking fast. Other messengers went out to summon the illustrious strangers. The Gospel goes on: "Then Herod privately calling the wise men, learned diligently of them the time of the star which appeared to them."

What a different company now appeared before King Herod! Not the submissive subjects of a dictator, always trembling in their boots, but free men, kings greeting a king. There was salaaming again, but this time it was on both sides, and the sick man on his golden couch tried very, very hard to be at his best. His shrewd, wicked mind was all made up. At his earliest opportunity he had to do away with that "King of the Jews" whom these magnificent-looking foreigners had come to adore, but first he must find out something about Him. They had said that they had seen His star. Very much depended now on the time. Herod feared that the star might have appeared to them many years ago, and this King of the Jews, the Messiah, might be a warrior now, ready to strike. That is why Herod "learned diligently of them the time of the star which appeared to them." What a sigh of relief when he learned the time! An ugly smile played around his cruel lips when he thought that his opponent was a mere Baby in His mother's arms. But he had to finish his act, and he played it well: "And sending them into Bethlehem, said: Go and diligently inquire after the child, and when you have found him, bring me word again, that I also may come and adore him."

With the childlike minds of the truly great they bowed and assured him that of course nothing would give them more pleasure; and with this promise the venerable men hurried to meet their caravan and be on the way, now that they knew where to go. "Wise men," the Gospel calls them, but Herod had outsmarted them, so it seemed, because "the children of this world are wiser in their generation than the children of light" (Luke 16:8).

"Who, having heard the king went their way; and behold the star which they had seen in the east went before them until it came and stood over where the child was. And seeing the star they rejoiced with exceeding great joy."

Only now, at the "exceeding great joy" with which they

see the star again after not having seen it for a while, only now can we imagine what a terrific trial Jerusalem must have been to those kingly souls: After their great decision to come all those vast distances, after the preparations and troubles and dangers of the journey, they finally reached the goal, the capital of the land of the Jews, and the palace of the king, where, of course, they expected the Infant to be. When they saw the perplexity on everybody's face when they asked the eager question: "Where is the new-born King of the Jews?" they grew more and more puzzled, and even the star had disappeared. Maybe this was the darkest hour in their lives. If the people at home had perhaps been startled at their whole undertaking, every word of their warnings must have come back now when it all seemed to be a failure. It is so very humanly possible that the temptation may have arisen to leave quietly before their embarrassing situation became too widely known. They must have felt ashamed and embarrassed and bitterly disappointed when they learned that for a long, long time there hadn't been a baby born in this royal palace of Jerusalem. But they were too unsophisticated and truly great just to leave quickly and quietly, turn the heads of their camels towards the east and vanish into the Syrian desert. They believed in the star and in the One Who had sent it, even after it had disappeared, and now—what a royal reward!

The moon had left Stowe Hollow and was now standing directly over Cor Unum, our house. On account of the snow all around us, there was a dim twilight in the room—and a deep silence.

"And?" said Hester finally.

"Oh, excuse me," I replied, "I couldn't help thinking of the time when our family felt some of this 'exceeding great joy.' That was when in our life the star reappeared, too."

Hester looked at me, and it was bright enough to see the questioning expression on her face, although she didn't say anything; so I explained.

"One day in our life as a family we saw a great big light just as the kings saw the star. It was the time when we saw clearly that we had to give up our material goods in order to save the spiritual ones; and as an entire family, father, mother, and nine children, leave our native Austria and become voluntary refugees. The few friends and relatives who heard about this were aghast and very much against it. When we finally, after many adventures, reached our Jerusalem, namely New York City, thinking now we had reached the goal, it looked all of a sudden like a complete failure. The star was gone. In our hearts resounded the words of our well-meaning friends about Hitler's promise of a thousand years of peace and the brilliant future our children could have had in his Third Reich—and there we were in America and nobody seemed to want us. It was a very dark hour. The war with Germany had not yet broken out. People urged us to go back; we would never be a success in this country. I shall never forget that particular hour. We were in the Hotel Wellington, my husband and I. It was past midnight and a gentleman had just left who for hours had tried to persuade us to go home on the next boat. When the door had closed behind him, I looked at my husband. We were both tired and very much discouraged. We had just enough money left to pay for our hotel, and there didn't seem to be any future.

"Then Georg said: 'We were so deeply convinced when we left Salzburg that this was the Will of God, and when one day we came through Cologne and knelt at the shrine of the three Holy Kings, we made them our patron saints for the time of our wanderings. Then we promised God to imitate them and persevere even if we couldn't see the star. I think this is the time now.'

"Still very tired, but not desparate any more, we went to bed. And then it all happened fast. We found the manager who understood us and in whose hands we felt safe as artists as well as people. 'And behold the star which they had seen in the east went before them. . . . And seeing the star, they rejoiced with exceeding great joy.'

"You see," I concluded my little digression, "the Gospel is still going on in our very own days, and if we only would let Him, Our Lord would re-live His life in each one of our lives all over again. Don't you know from your own past the times when the star has seemingly vanished, and don't you know this 'exceeding great joy' when it appears again?''

"I think I know what you mean," said Hester, and she seemed to know what she was talking about. "And?" she added, which made me conscious that I hadn't finished my story of the three Holy Kings yet.

It must have become rather late by now, because, in the house below, one after the other of the lighted windows was darkened.

"Don't let's look at the watch, but let's finish," I resolved.

When they had passed through the city gate, they had to go directly south for five miles. This is now something for our imagination to dwell on: the long caravan, really three caravans merged in one, the many camels with their bells, the swift horses, the stately elephants—for each king had come on the animals of his country—and a big star traveling above them in the air, enveloping them all in a soft light. How they must all have looked up to the star gliding along before them and thanked God from the depths of their hearts. After five miles the road turned sharply to the left, and there they saw Bethlehem, the little town perched on the hillside—like Assisi—in the midst of vineyards and olive groves, surrounded by big sheep pastures. The star traveled right into town and stopped above a house. There was no doubt: now they had reached their destination. Camels and elephants dropped to their knees, horses stood still, and the next moment the Magi-Kings had dismounted and were now beckoning to their servants. This was a sign which they well understood, and the kings were brought the gifts which were intended for the newborn King of the Jews. In the East it was the custom to give a present to any superior as a sign of respect. We see that repeatedly in the Old Testament. Now St. Matthew tells us: "And opening their treasures, they offered him gifts: gold, frankincense, and myrrh."

On this very day St. Joseph must not have been at home. He was most probably at work somewhere because "they found the child with Mary his mother." And now something quaint happens: "And falling down they adored him." Little Jesus was obviously sitting on His mother's lap, and His mother, the most humble handmaid of the Lord, accepted the homage of these venerable men with complete composure. She did not stop them, she did not interrupt their adoration with polite words. She knew that falling down and prostrating was a tribute given only to God, and Mary accepted it for the little King. Later Our Lord would exclaim several times: "Amen . . . I have not found so great faith in Israel" (Matt. 8:10), always talking about one or the other Gentile. If the little Child could have talked, He would have said the same right then. The Sanhedrin, the official lawgiving body, had formally announced that "the Christ is to be born in Bethlehem," and everybody understood that this little Child the high-born strangers from the Orient had come to worship must be identical with Him. It is one of the greatest riddles that the Sanhedrists just seem to have returned to their homes from their summons to the king, and no one—no Pharisee, no Saducee, no Rabbi, none of the elders seems to have taken any action at all concerning the Child only a few miles away in Bethlehem. Some of them *must* have heard some rumors of the birth in the cave with the manger, of the Gloria in Excelsis, of the talk of Simeon and Anna—it is just incredible and unbelieving that nothing, absolutely nothing was done until the pagans, the Gentiles, prostrated themselves before Him and presented Him with gifts.

St. Bede the Vnerable says: "The first is said to have been Melchior, a bald man with a long beard and hair, who offered gold to the King and Lord" (princes from the East always honored their sovereigns with a gift of gold). The second, Caspar, was a beardless young man of a ruddy hue, and he came with frankincense, the most expensive fragrance of the East, always considered too precious to use for humans, and always reserved for the temples. Caspar honored in the little Child—God. Then came Balthasar, the dark one. His vessel of myrrh reminds us of the story of his people, grand but sad, myrrh used for the embalming of the dead. Never again in His whole life will Our Lord be offered gold or frankincense, but twice He will be offered myrrh: on the cross by the soldiers, and after His death, by Nicodemus. Strangely enough, His mother will receive it from Nicodemus, as she receives it now from Balthasar.

After the official homage was paid in prostration and presenting of gifts, Mary got up, I am sure, and showed her precious little Child to her noble guests. Each one was allowed to take Him in his arms and look at His smiling little face. It must have been the happiest moment of their lives.

Then with their hearts full to the brim, they must have asked the mother questions and Mary, who will be asked questions by another Gentile later and will tell all the wondrous secrets to him who will put them down as the Gospel of St. Luke, Mary might have told these great and venerable souls the story of the Annunciation and what the angel said, the story of the Visitation and what Elizabeth said, the story of the Nativity and what the shepherds said. Then it was time for her royal guests to leave. And now I remember something which I read years ago. Theresa Neumann of Konnersreuth telling about her vision of the visit of the three Holy Kings, says that after they left the house, they took the mother and the little Boy with them to show the Child around the camp with the gorgeous Persian carpet tents and all those strange animals, and little Jesus, just over a year old, was happily walking between camels, which were ordered to lie down and take Him on their humps, and elephants, which tenderly placed Him on their heads with their trunks, while the ravishingly beautiful girl-mother watched His great delight with a smile.

"Well—this is the way Theresa Neumann saw it, and it may not be the historic truth; but it is not at all impossible, and don't you think, Hester, it is lovely?"

"Yes!" said she wholeheartedly.

What a horror to think that at the same time the old dying man in Jerusalem with one foot in the grave was already preparing his soldiers to kill this beautiful young Boy, Who was now clapping His little hands and having the time of His life!

When St. Joseph came home from work that evening, Mary told him about the wondrous happenings of the day and showed him the gifts. To the mind of the silent man must have come the words of the Seventy-first Psalm: "All kings of the earth shall adore, and all nations shall serve him." And then although they didn't know it, they spent their last quiet evening for a long, long time to come. The little Boy had been put to bed. Mary and Joseph went and looked at the gold, frankincense, and myrrh.

Caspar, Melchior, and Balthasar could hardly go to sleep with so much happiness throbbing in their hearts. When their tired eyes had closed in slumber, an angel of the Lord came to them with a message from on High: they were not to return to Herod.

What a consolation to us when the children of the world all around us are getting smarter all the time! In Compline we say every Sunday: "For he hath given his angels charge over thee, to keep thee in all thy ways. In their hands they shall bear thee up, lest thou dash thy foot against a stone" (Ps. 90:11-12).

One can't help wondering whether this angel, having given his message, turned right around and went over to "the house" where he also had to deliver a message.

Caspar, Melchior, and Balthasar would get up quietly, order their camp to be broken up quickly, and instead of going north to Jerusalem, they would head straight east, ford the Jordan, and in a couple of hours be across the border out of the reach of Herod. The mysterious East would swallow them up.

Tradition has it that after the Apostle Thomas had baptized them, they in turn tried to preach Christianity in their countries, but met with so much hostility that they soon died for their Lord and King. The early Christians venerated them as martyrs.

Now the moon was looking directly into our window.

"When we go to Europe next year," Hester asked, "shall we stop at Cologne?"

"Oh, let us hope so," I said, and we walked down through the deep snow. The house was all dark now. Only the moon and the stars had witnessed the story which had warmed our hearts for the last hours.

IX

the fugitive

In the beginning of this book I told "how it happened." "It" means that we as a family became so much interested in the life of Christ that we started to rebuild it for ourselves, to re-live it day by day. After a few years of doing this, and as we knew Him better and better, we began to feel very close to Him. Finally He was not only a good friend; more and more He had become like one of us—a member of our family. As it had all begun with my telling my crying little girl the story of the Flight into Egypt, this story has always remained a favorite among us. We have tried ever so hard to collect all that is known about it, and on top of this, use our family imagination. By now it has grown like this:

While in Bethlehem the two little groups of three holy persons each, the Holy Family and the Holy Kings, finally fell into peaceful slumber, Herod in near-by Jerusalem was very restless. For one thing, he could not sleep because of the awful disease which was eating him up; but on this night something else kept him awake—the thought of his innocent little rival. With growing impatience he awaited the return of the three kings. These star-gazers—would they never come?

Little did he know that just now in the middle of the night the course of those "star-gazers" had been changed, and they were already on their way far from him. He, of course, had expected them back the same evening, maybe late at night, and now the hours were dragging on, and he worked himself more and more into one of his paroxysms of wrath. The mere idea that this hated Child should escape him drove him into fury.

In the early dawn of morning he shouted his commands, which he had changed from murdering just one little Boy living in a certain house, to killing every male child up to two years, to be absolutely sure *He* was among them. Herod had three companies of mercenaries: Galatians, Thracians, and Teutons. On these brutal soldiers he could depend to execute any command, however bloody, even against the members of his own family. A stiff march of an hour and a half took them to Bethlehem, where they began at once to scatter, searching the houses, butchering the baby boys in their mothers' arms, and before the little town had fully awakened to what had happened, the soldiers were already on their way back. The shrieks of the inconsolable mothers rose to heaven: "A voice in Rama was heard, lamentation and great mourning; Rachel bewailing her children . . ." (Matt. 2:18).

How many little boys were killed? It is said that Bethlehem had a thousand inhabitants at that time. The number of births in a year was about thirty. In two years, therefore, there would be sixty; and if half of them were girls, it would leave thirty boys. In those times, however, there was quite a high rate of infant mortality, so maybe there were no more than twenty.

The little bodies lay in their blood, while their parents were completely overwhelmed with grief. The Church tells us in the liturgy on the Feast of the Holy Innocents, December 28, that the Heavenly Father looked upon these innocent souls as the first martyrs who had given their blood for His Son.

After St. Matthew finishes his story about the three wise men, "And having received an answer in sleep that they should not return to Herod, they went back another way into their country," he continues: "And after they were departed, behold an angel of the Lord appeared in sleep to Joseph, saying; Arise, and take the child and his mother and fly into Egypt: and be there until I shall tell thee. For it will come to pass that Herod will seek the child to destroy him'' (Matt. 2:12-13).

''And after they were departed,'' the Gospel says, so obviously, Caspar, Melchior, and Balthasar first disappeared with their caravan and were swallowed up by the darkness of the night when the angel came to Joseph with the command: ''Arise.'' This meant immediate danger. These words of the Gospel might never have been so widely and so fully understood since they were written down, as they were by millions and millions of people all over Europe and all over the encroaching realm of the Iron Curtain: ''The Communists are coming—arise and flee!'' What Herod was to his time, a tyrant, Lenin and Stalin are to our days. They all have one thing in common: They have no use for ''the Christ.'' Now as then, they seek to destroy Him. Therefore, the angel goes also through our days, or rather nights, and the ''arise and flee'' is heard by millions. That is why our times seem perhaps closer than any of the nineteen centuries to the very beginnings of Christianity. Whenever refugees are fleeing because their Christian faith is threatened—all over the highways and byways of Poland, Germany, Austria, Czechoslovakia, Hungary, in the Balkans, or in China—they never have to feel alone. In them Our Lord Jesus Christ, the same yesterday as today, is still on His flight into Egypt.

Joseph, tired though he was from his day's work, must have been immediately wide awake upon hearing the word ''Arise and take the child and his mother.'' With a heavy heart he wakened Mary, who was so peacefully asleep together with her Baby, trusting so completely in his protection. When Mary recognized his voice and understood what he said, she arose—I almost said hastily, but no, that would not be right. I am absolutely sure that in her whole life she never did anything hastily. Everything she did and the very way she did it must always have been just right because she was so completely anchored in God. She just rose quickly, very quickly. And the handmaid of the

Lord kept her head again as she had done when the great angel appeared in Nazareth, when Elizabeth had said such outstanding things, and when Simeon's message tore her heart. In no time she had wrapped up the little Boy tenderly and taken the few things she would need; for poverty doesn't take long to pack. The only really valuable things they owned were the gifts of the kings. Joseph must have wrapped them carefully. Maybe in less than ten minutes they had quietly left the house. The donkey they came on from Nazareth must still have been around, and Joseph lifted Mary with the sleeping Child in her arms on its back.

We feel it now as a great privelege to have been refugees once, to know what anxiety means. The clatter of the donkey's hooves on the cobblestones of Bethlehem, for instance: wouldn't that wake up somebody who might report them later? That's why they hurried down the slope into the vineyards and fields to get away as fast as possible. Every sound arouses one's fears. "Maybe they have found out and are on our heels"—that's the constant fear. When the sky grew light, the first cocks began to crow, and the horrid battalion entered the small town, perhaps Mary and Joseph, who were slow travelers, might still have heard the shrieks which rent the air and sent cold chills down their backs. They were still very close to Herod's power. They were still in the neighborhood where they might have been known and identified. . . .

Oh, it is so wrong to picture the Flight into Egypt as a nice, smooth hike with angels on all sides ministering to them. The angels certainly were there admiring, adoring, almost unbelieving that the Lord would not have protected His only-begotten Son by means less troublesome than this pitiful flight. Where was the Angel of Death who slew the Egyptians? Where was the angel with the fiery sword at the gates of paradise? But it was obviously the Will of the Most High—that the Child and His mother be saved not by supernatural interference, but by the natural means of a tedious flight. We people living in the middle of the twentieth century understand perhaps a little better why: He really has become "like one of us," and we can go

to Him also during a flight or a persecution, saying
full of confidence: "You know how it is."

The books say that there were two main routes going
from Judea into Egypt. It is interesting now to look them
up on the map. The more popular route was "the way of
the land of the Philistines" (Exod. 13:17), via Ascalon and
Gaza and then along the shore of the Mediterranean towards the delta of the Nile. The other way led through
Hebron and Beersheba to the land on the Nile and was
called "the way to Sur in the desert" (Gen. 16:7).Every
refugee will tell you that if one wants to get away from
feared territory as quickly and safely as possible, one uses
the less-traveled routes. That's why they must have gone
south to Hebron about fifteen miles. It has been ascer-
tained that "the ordinary rate for a long journey on foot
was about seventeen Roman miles per day" (Hastings'
Dictionary of the Bible), so the Holy Family could have
reached Hebron that first day. Every refugee will also
tell you that you don't stay overnight in a town even
if it should be dear to you because it contains the tomb of
your own ancestors (like Hebron, where Father Abraham
had buried his beloved wife, Sarah); so they hurried on.
Farther south about twenty miles was an oasis, the famous
Beersheba, the southernmost settlement in Palestine. Did
Mary and Joseph talk about the fact that from here Father
Abraham had set out to sacrifice his only son, that here
also he had pushed Agar and Ishmael into the wilderness?
Here Joseph must have filled their water bags, because
now they were setting out into the barren desert. Beyond
Beersheba they could afford to breathe a little more freely
because they were out of Herod's immediate jurisdiction,
but they were still in the Roman Province of Syria. You
never could tell whether Herod had perhaps gotten the
Romans to lend him a hand. Therefore, Mary and Joseph
would keep hurrying on towards the river Rhinocolura.
After having passed the frontier between Syria and Egypt,
they did relax somewhat, but now came the worst stretch
of the journey, more than a hundred miles of unbroken
desert.

When we were on the way to California in our big blue bus, we saw for the first time in our lives real desert with sand dunes. Because of our favorite Gospel, we asked the driver to stop on the highway and we, taking our shoes and stockings off, waded into the dunes, thinking that the sandals of antiquity were not much more protection than going barefoot because the hot sand would be constantly between the soles and the leather. I remember so vividly how we couldn't stand it more than ten minutes, hastening back to the bus with a stinging sensation all over our legs which lasted the rest of the day. And this was in early spring, and the desert was not yet at its hottest. It certainly gave us first-hand experience of how those three hundred sixty miles between Bethlehem and Heliopolis must have been. The books say that in those times little ones were nursed by their mothers for a full two years. Every mother knows that during the time of nursing one wants to drink a great deal. The water in the skins had to be dished out very sparingly. He who would later feed five thousand and another time four thousand by a miracle, didn't do a thing to help Himself or His mother and foster father, although a wave of his little hand would have turned the desert into paradise.

There are many lovely legends woven around this flight through the desert. Painters throughout the centuries have taken hold of them, and we see Mary resting peacefully on a green carpet of grass while Joseph is picking apples and the Infant is playing with young lions. In another picture we see little Jesus beckoning to a group of tall date palms, they bending down so that He can pick what He wants, or the animals of the desert coming to their aid and the Holy Family riding on zebras, giraffes, and lions. The loveliest of all these stories, however, is the one true version that nothing of the extraordinary happened and they had to take every step through the hot sand by themselves, shiver through the cold nights, fear the robbers and the wild animals, be hungry, thirsty and tired—oh, so tired— and that they did it for us, for you and me. Since we discovered this story when we were just beginning as refugees, it has warmed our hearts, it has made us feel good in that company!

Finally the weary wanderers saw before them the many waters of the Nile, the green and lush delta. Tradition has it that they went to Heliopolis. In order to get there they must have passed through many towns before, through well-irrigated fields, finally passing obelisks and pyramids. Mary and Joseph must have talked about the role Egypt had played in the history of their people. Abraham had fled there once in time of famine, and another Joseph had been taken there by force, which was another *felix culpa*, because at his invitation he finally got his whole clan into the land. For the next four hundred years they would be first the guests of the Pharoah and later his slaves until God would awaken Moses to lead them away into the Promised Land. About all this Mary and Joseph must have talked, and many times they must have recited together the psalms which dealt with captivity and hardship and the Heavenly Father finally leading them out into green pastures.

One of the glories of doing this particular story from the Gospels as a family is that one really learns so much about Egypt. The different children in their different grades can now contribute what they know about the old Egyptians and how they lived. For the parents school days are re-awakened. One looks up old history books, and pooling it all, it is amazing what a good picture one can get of the Holy Family in Egypt! The most striking part of this story will be when it comes to the religion of the Egyptians. The books say that at the time of Christ the religion of the Egyptians had deteriorated into worshiping animals themselves: crocodiles, snakes, birds, cows, cats, and rams, if they were born of one solid color. The books also say that many Jews had settled in Egypt, and in the big cities like Alexandria, Heliopolis, or Memphis, the population was about two thirds Jewish. In Heliopolis there was a Jewish colony. That's where the Holy Family found refuge. Now they were in the true sense of the word Displaced Persons with no plans of their own, waiting to see what would be done with them. "Be there," had the angel said, "until I shall tell thee."

"If-ing it," or "perhaps-ing it" means in our family try-ing out different possible ways of how it might have been. "Perhaps," therefore, Joseph used the gold of Melchior to rent a house and get the necessary things to set up a humble household—this was never to be home; this would always be exile.

Now Joseph would find himself work, and Mary would keep house. They were not rich enough to afford a baby sitter, so whenever she went shopping in the bazaar, she would take her little Boy with her, and it is perfectly possi-ble that many a time she must have witnessed how the street crier came along making room for a sacred cow or a sacred cat, ordering everyone prostrate in the dust. Of course, Mary would never obey this command. The people would curse the Jewish swine, as they used to say in mockery because the Jews did not touch any pork. There she stood pressed against the wall until the dull-looking animal had slowly passed, holding by the hand Him Who would once exclaim: "I am the light of the world" (John 8:12). "That was the true light, which en-lighteneth every man that cometh into this world," St. John would start out his Gospel. "He was in the world: and the world was made by him: and the world knew him not. He came unto his own: and his own received him not." Even if they were out of immediate danger from Herod, they must always have felt very bitterly to see how far the people around them had drifted away from God.

According to ancient tradition the Holy Family went from Heliopolis to Memphis and stayed there for the rest of the time. There those things must have happened which make the heart of every young mother warm with joy. At His mother's knee little Jesus would begin to talk and sing little songs. From her He was learning His first prayers and listening to His first stories. Now there is no end of "perhaps-ing": Which were His first words, which the first prayers, and what kind of stories? This depends a little bit on the question of how long the Holy Family stayed in Egypt. The Fathers of the Church are of different opinions. St. Bonaventure believed that they stayed in Egypt as long as seven years. Then the stories would most certainly be all those beautiful Bible stories, which in His case were at the same time family history. In the young Heart would awaken homesickness for His Father's House, where the mother had dwelt for many years, and which she could describe so wonderfully. Like every refugee child, He would grow up on the stories of how it was in the "old country," which He Himself can't remember beause He was too small at the time of flight, but which fill His little Heart with nostalgia.

There is one old tradition which has it that because Joseph was not earning enough, Mary would do very fine and beautiful embroidery for rich Egyptian ladies, some of which is still kept as a most precious relic.

Besides all the hardships and all the nostalgia, there is one more emotion which fills a refugee's heart, and that is deep gratitude to his hosts for their hospitality. He wants to repay in whatever small measure he can. Christ repaid Egypt in His own inimitable hundred-fold ways; In the course of time its cities would be filled with bishops and saints, the wildnerness around would swarm with the fathers of the desert. St. John Chrysostom would say of the Egypt of his own time in the fourth century: "And shouldst thou come now into the desert of Egypt, thou wilt see this desert become better than any paradise, and ten thousand choirs of angels in human forms, whole nations of martyrs and companies of virgins, and all the devil's tyranny put down while Christ's Kingdom shines forth in its brightness" (Hom. 8 on Matt.).

Every refugee is just living for the day when he can return home, so finally the glorious moment arrived when "Behold an angel of the Lord appeared in sleep to Joseph in Egypt saying: Arise and take the child and his mother and go into the land of Israel, for they are dead that sought the life of the child. Who arose and took the child and his mother and came into the land of Israel."

Upon this, invariably, one of the children will ask:

"Why again at night? Why arise and take the Child and His mother? Couldn't they just leave normally like any other travelers, join a caravan and have it a little easier?" Well, this is one of those questions which we still haven't found an answer to.

One of our children asked once: "Mother if the three Holy Kings had to leave the same night, couldn't they have taken the Holy Family on their camels? Don't you think they would have enjoyed doing this, and just think how much easier for Mary and Joseph!" It had never occurred to me before, but it was a good suggestion, and there was no question of *how* they would have liked to do this. At least one of them had to go in that direction anyhow. The one from Ethiopia had to pass through Egypt to go home. The only answer is that the other was the Will of the Heavenly Father.

How light-hearted they must have been on the long and hard journey back, reciting over and over again Psalm 121: "I rejoiced at the things that were said to me: We shall go into the house of the Lord." They were heading for Bethlehem. It might not be impossible that on one of these days the thought occurred to Mary that her little Jesus would have no playmates of His own age. The boys in Bethlehem would be either a little older or a little younger than He. Towards the very end of the trip, however, Joseph got another one of his nightly messages: He should not go to Bethlehem in Judea because the successor of Herod was not much better than Herod himself, but he should go into Galilee. So they chose the home town of the mother and went to Nazareth and settled there.

X

"unless you . . . become as little children"

A grave injustice is done to Mary, and to Jesus her Son if we do not take them as real people, persons like you and me, completely alike in everything — except sin. Isn't Jesus for most of us most of our lives—and I mean now humanly speaking—some kind of superman? And Mary, well—she is a myth, something of the same kind, very much to be admired, but definitely not someone whom you would take into your home, whom you would ask to live with you, no more than you would invite a member of foreign royalty. You would feel too awkward, to uncomfortable. All the ease would be gone from your home, as if one couldn't smoke or relax in a chair in their presence, talk small talk about the household, the high prices of nowadays, the threatening danger of war, as long as they are around. What a great, great pity, and how very wrong! Still—isn't this the way it is with the majority of Christians nowadays? And why? Only because we don't know them. What do we know, for instance, about the so-called Hidden Life? I dread this very expression "Hidden Life," because these two words seem to have had a queer influence on us. Most of thirty years of the life of Christ is covered by this expression which we have learned to accept as a fact. Just because the Gospels don't say a word about what was going on, we seem to have taken the attitude that one doesn't know or couldn't know anything that was going on in the Holy Family, and so we deprive ourselves of living His *whole* life with Him. The years of

His childhood until He became of age as a "son of the law," the years from twelve to twenty when He had reached majority in His tribe, the precious years from twenty to thirty when He was a grown-up Man like our brothers and our husbands. But we people of 1952 cannot do that any longer. There are these books like the *Bible Encyclopedia* in one volume or *Mary the Mother of Jesus* by Reverend Franz M. William or the books by Father O'Shea and others which will help us reconstruct the daily life of the Holy Family almost as easily as we might reconstruct the daily life of our great-grandmothers.

St. Luke (2:39-40) says: "They returned into Galilee, to their city Nazareth. And the child grew and waxed strong, full of wisdom: and the grace of God was in him." And because nothing spectacular happened until He was twelve years old, there isn't anything more said but that they returned to Nazareth. The Evangelist might have felt foolish if he had gone into an exact description of what they did there day by day, year after year, because all his contemporaries knew that anyhow; and if we don't know it any more, it's our own fault. It is only due to lack of interest, to the greatest sin of all, indifference; because while we are interested enough, we know how and where to find information on, for instance, how the Pharaohs in Egypt lived, just exactly how they embalmed their mummies, how the aborigines live in Tierra del Fuego. It costs just as much effort to find out about the customs of Palestine at the time of Christ; and if we don't know these things, if we don't know, for instance, which daily prayers were said in the Holy Family, how the Sabbath was observed, what the school system was like at that time in the Holy Land, what the position of the mother was in the house—well then we must soberly admit that we are more interested in the pygmies and the old Egyptians than in the daily life of Our Lord.

Indifference was the sin which hurt Our Lord most, and with which He was most impatient: "I would thou wert cold or hot. But because thou art lukewarm and neither cold nor hot, I will begin to vomit thee out of my mouth"

(Apoc. 3:15-16). If we are not in a position to know for ourselves one complete day in the Holy Family from dawn to dusk, or one week from Sabbath to Sabbath, or one year with the major feasts and pilgrimages to Jerusalem, if we don't know down to details the political situation of Our Lord's country and people during His own time, if we don't know the mountains and valleys, the cities and villages and what they looked like, the change of seasons, the flowers and animals—if we don't know this, then we have to admit with a sorry heart that we have sinned gravely through indifference. And there is only one thing to do: Get to work right away.

Very soon the Hidden Life will not be hidden at all when we see Mary busy in her household from morning till night: starting out early at dawn carrying the day's supply of water, not only for drinking and cooking, but also for the liturgical ablutions, from the well into her house in an earthen pitcher on her head; then grinding the day's portion of meal and baking their daily bread, taking a broom and sweeping the house, preparing the meals, spinning flax and wool, and weaving undergarments, tunics and mantles, one for the Sabbath and holy days, another one for every day. And when we learn in detail how these things were done—very soon we shall lose this notion that Mary spent her life with eyes raised and hands folded in prayer. She will become a woman of flesh and blood, a mother and housewife; and very soon we shall find ourselves talking things over with her, things which pertain to household and children, the elements of women's talk all over the world. And by "talking things over," we shall have started out on a new life of prayer hitherto unknown to us. We might never use the word "meditation," but we shall meditate, or the word "contemplation," but we shall experience the fact that enough meditation automatically leads to quiet contemplation. Jesus and Mary will not only not be strangers any more, but they will really become members of our household, more so perhaps than some of our very own relatives, an uncle or an aunt whom we don't see very often.

Let us start out right away. "They returned into Galilee, to their city Nazareth." This return may not have been of unmixed joy. Nazareth was a provincial town where everybody knows everybody. Mary and Joseph had left it years ago. Now they came back with the little Boy, a few years old. Don't you think all the neighbors would want to know where they had been and what they had been doing all the time?

"In Egypt? No, not really! But why?" Small town gossip was waiting for them.

Then the daily life began with Joseph the father of the house. In the eyes of men it was Joseph, Mary, Jesus, while in the eyes of God it was Jesus, Mary, Joseph. Joseph opened his carpenter shop and began to work for his livelihood. In his work shop he made implements like plows, pieces of furniture such as chests and low tables; he also went out putting roofs of cedar beams on houses. One thing he never, never did, which our holy cards have adopted and seem to like so much—he never made a cross. This was the most hated gallows which the Romans had brought into the country. While Joseph was busy at his craft, Mary, the "valiant woman . . . hath put out her hand to strong things, and her fingers have taken hold of the spindle. . . . She hath looked well to the paths of her house, and hath not eaten her bread idle" (Prov. 31:10, 19, 27).

What was Jesus doing when He was seven, eight, nine, ten, eleven years old? He was watching His mother and foster father, and very soon He would imitate them. Soon He would find out that on one day in the week there was a completely different atmosphere around the house. This Holy Day began early the night before. It lasted from sunset to sunset. The work shop would be closed, they would wear their Sabbath clothes, the mother would not cook, but they would eat what she had prepared the day before. The house was especially carefully swept and cleaned. It was the duty of the mother of every house to light the "Sabbath Lamp." Jesus would see His mother do it in her inimitable reverent, loving way, spreading out her hands before the lamp, pronouncing the benediction: "Blessed art Thou,

oh Lord our God, King of the universe, Who hast sancti-
fied us by Thy commandments and commanded us to
kindle the Sabbath Lamp.'' Then as long as the Boy was
small, He would see Joseph leave with quick steps and
later on return in a markedly different way, slowly and
thoughtfully. His mother would explain to Him that the
Rabbis had pronounced this as the way to go to and from
church, as we would say. The food was what we would call
a Sunday dinner. Aren't we interested in finding out what
they ate, how it was prepared, and how it was served? If we
look at our map, we see Nazareth not very far from the big
lake. We know that there were many fishermen. Fish was
eaten much more than meat, especially in a small family.
A levitical law commanded the eating of a whole animal at
once. That is why lambs, kids and calves, eggs and cheese
were preferred to beef. Besides, meat was expensive, and
the Holy Family, as we still remember from their behavior in the temple when they couldn't afford the lamb,
belonged to what we would call the middle class, not rich
and not destitute. They were poor, but not to the extent
of misery. Mary and Joseph always made ends meet. But
there were no luxuries around.

The work shop must have been a child's paradise for the
little Boy. What grand toys there were just lying around
on the floor!

Then one day He must have begun to accompany His
mother to the well. There He heard the women greeting
each other with the beautiful word, *"Shalom"* (Peace).
This well still exists. We can show pictures of it to our
children.

Jesus was a healthy, normal Boy. As such, He would
want to play with other boys. The time would come when
He would be allowed to go out with them and explore the
neighborhood.

And He had to go to school. That was commanded by
the law. The Rabbis even forbade the people to settle in
a place where there was no school! School was usually connected with the Synagogue, and we know from the Gospels
that there was a Synagogue in Nazareth. Only the boys

went to school, and there they learned to read, but not to write. Two books they were taught: the Torah, which is known to us as the Law of the Old Testament, and the Mishnah, a commentary to it, the teachings of the famous Rabbis. In a small circle the little boys sat on the floor before their teacher, who would teach them first orally by saying a sentence and having them repeat, repeat, repeat. After they really knew it by heart, then he showed them the script. This was so much the method of the day that the verbs "to teach" and "to learn" were identical with the verb "to repeat." The little ones were not only taught the verses of Holy Scriptures, but they were also taught practical things like behavior, moral conduct, etiquette. And so, Jesus went to school, like my Johannes and your Tom or Jim. And Mary and Joseph were just as anxious as you and I as to whether He made progress, and He always did.

St. Luke says: "And the child grew and waxed strong, full of wisdom: and the grace of God was in him," The same St. Luke who said now the child was "full of wisdom," would say on the next page that He "advanced in wisdom and age and grace with God and men" (Luke 2:52). Here we come upon something which we cannot explain by mere study of history, geography, or sociology. Here we come across one of the deepest mysteries of our religion, something which is a divine secret and would never have been found out by men if it hadn't been for divine revelation. You and I can attain to three kinds of knowledge: there is a knowledge we get in a natural way. This is the usual experimental knowledge which we pick up as we grow. Then some people, usually the saints, have also infused knowledge. That means knowing, like the prophets, for instance, things which they couldn't possibly have learned in a natural way. And then you and I will one day be capable of still another knowledge when we shall meet God face to face in the Beatific Vision. And now it is such a marvel to think: From the very first moment of His existence on earth Our Lord Jesus Christ enjoyed this Beatific Vision. He always saw the Father face to face. He also possessed all this intuitive, infused knowledge. Isaias knew that already when he prophesied about Him: "And the spirit of the Lord shall rest upon him: the spirit of wisdom, and of understanding, the spirit of counsel, and of fortitude, the spirit of knowledge and of godliness" (Isa. 11:2). Since Jesus possessed it all—always —in these two knowledges He could not grow. And then, oh wonder, He is a little Boy like yours and mine, Who can grow in wisdom and grace before God and men. This unique mystery can never be explained, it can only be believed. Because Jesus had two natures, a human nature and a divine nature in one person, He could advance humanly while he was always in God, with God—while He *was* God. Our theologians call this the Hypostatic Union.

Just what did that mean now in His daily life? Why don't we begin to ponder about it in our hearts? We shall never be finished, but we have all eternity to continue.

These are the precious years up to His twelfth birthday when Jesus was a Child. Our children wanted to know whether they observed birthdays and feast days and other anniversaries in the Holy Family. After some thinking we decided: they must have, because Mary and Joseph both understood to the fullest extent what those days really meant in the history of mankind: when the angel asked Mary whether she would agree to be the mother of the Messiah and she answered her immortal, "Behold the hand-maid of the Lord," when "the light shone in the darkness" in the cave outside of Bethlehem. They saw these days as days of tremendous grace which the Heavenly Father poured out over His undeserving children. In filial gratitude Mary must always have celebrated the anniversaries, and so in the first Christian families they celebrated just privately among themselves birthdays, holidays, and anniversaries like that of the Annunciation, Visitation, Presentation.

Let us come back to the thought that Jesus was a real Child. Much later He will one day solemnly declare to us how we have to be and what we have to do if we want to go to heaven. He will say it in His straightforward, unsophisticated, unmistakable way when He takes a little boy, pointing to him and saying: "Amen I say to you, unless you be converted and become as little children, you shall not enter into the kingdom of heaven" (Matt. 18:3). Just like that: "If you don't, then you won't." There is absolutely nothing we can do about it, but one day we have to face this phrase and what it means. We get a certain help in how we have to take it when we think of another incident when Our Lord talked to one of the most sophisticated intellectuals of his day, Nicodemus, a member of the Sanhedrin. When Our Lord said to him: "Amen, amen, I say to thee, unless a man be born again, he cannot see the kingdom of God," Nicodemus, the typical grownup, said, stupefied: "How can a man be born when he is old? Can he enter a second time into his mother's womb and be born again?" This brought him a slightly ironical: "Art thou a master in Israel, and knowest not these things?" (John 3:3-4, 10) from Jesus, Who continues to explain that He certainly didn't think of the physical aspect of being born again, but. . . . So when He says: "Unless . . . you become as little children," this is a parallel, and we are not supposed to ask in the same stupefied way: "How can I become small again after I have grown up?" We know He doesn't mean that. So we face the necessity of having to do research work on the question: "What are children?" In what ways do children differ from grownups mentally and spiritually, if the physical comparison is to be disregarded but the word still stands: "Unless you become . . . " And we are about to make one of the most beautiful discoveries, urged on by the reading of the Gospels.

The most striking difference between little ones and grownups is that little ones cannot worry, and they cannot worry because they have no past and no future. They live only in the present moment. Just let us watch children. If they play, they play, and don't even hear us call them and don't notice anything that is going on around them. If they eat, they eat; if they sleep, they sleep. There is a beautiful English word which describes how they do whatever they do' they do it "whole-heartedly," whereas grownups always .

are half-hearted. While they do one thing, they have to worry about the past: "Oh, I should never have . . ., oh, if I only had . . ."; of the future: "My, and what is going to happen when . . ., and what will I do or what will I say if . . ." So they are in the true sense of the word split personalities and can never do anything with their whole heart. That's why that grave word is spoken over them: they cannot go to heaven because they cannot fulfill the first and most important commandment, which Our Lord said was: "Thou shalt love the Lord thy God with thy whole heart, and with they whole soul, and with thy whole mind" (Matt. 22:37). Only children or childlike souls can do anything with their whole heart. That's the first and most tremendous lesson.

Then we find a few more things. Children are full of confidence. They have not learned yet to be suspicious, and when they stretch out their little arms, what else can you do but take them up?

Or: Children learn by observing and imitating. Before they go to school they have learned a whole language and all the necessary ways of acting and doing in order to go through life: how to eat, how to sleep. . . . They watch the ones they love and trust, father and mother, sisters and brothers. If Our Lord wants us to be like little children in this regard, He certainly has supplied the means: He has told us about the Father in Heaven. We have the example of His wonderful mother and of all our older sisters and brothers, the saints. We have plenty to watch and imitate. There is just one hitch to it. Even the nicest little boy (or girl as far as that goes) will have his faults. Even the greatest saint will first have had to do an enormous amount of work to become like one of those little ones. But there we have Jesus in the first twelve years of His life when He was also in stature a Child, the holy Child, the perfect Child. And the greatest beauty is now that mentally He will not change—the one-ness of purpose, the whole-heartedness with which we see Him do everything, the complete absence of even an ability to worry in His character, His watching the Father and imitating Him, as He tells us in the Gospel of St. John. How truly can He say one day: "For I have given you an example, that as I have done to you, so you do also" (John 13:15).

In His great understanding of human nature He uses the word "become"; "unless you become as little children . . ." He knows that the way of the world is this: A little one is hardly out of the diapers when he is told approvingly: "But now you are a big boy." When he goes to kindergarten: "Now you are not a baby any more." When he is in the first grade: "Well, you are not in kindergarten any more; you are a big boy now." This goes on until in high school he doesn't have to be told that he is a big boy now. He knows it himself. Then one day sooner or later he will be banged on the head by those words of Our Lord, and all the growing up will not seem like an achievement any longer, but like something which has to be undone. That is when the "becoming" starts. After we have grown up in the eyes of the world, we have to "grow down" in the eyes of God. We have to. There is no way out as long as we want to go to heaven. Heaven is full of children; Our Lord Himself said so. One of the quickest ways for this "growing down" is to become very much at home in the little house in Nazareth—to watch and to imitate.

XI

"Did you not know . . . ?"

St. Luke says: "And his parents went every year to Jerusalem, at the solemn day of the pasch. And when he was twelve years old, they going up into Jerusalem, according to the custom of the feast . . ." (Luke 2:41-42).

We are more or less used to accepting the idea of their taking Him with them to the temple obviously for the first time as we might take our little ones for the first time with us to church. It is very much worth while to look at the map and to find out a few things about these pilgrimages which the Jewish men were obliged to make. There were three major feasts, about which the Book of Deuteronomy 16:16-17, says: "Three times in a year shall all thy males appear before the Lord thy God . . . in the feast of unleavened bread, in the feast of weeks, and in the feast of tabernacles. No one shall appear with his hands empty before the Lord. But every one shall offer according to what he hath. . . ."

The greatest of these feasts was the Pasch, the Feast of Unleavened Bread. The very word "Pasch" meant "Passover," as this feast was instituted in order to remind the Jews throughout all generations of that unforgettable night when the Angel of Death had passed over the houses of the Israelites in Egypt, whose doorposts had been smeared with the blood of a lamb. That is why a lamb had to be offered at the Pasch, and it had to be offered in Jerusalem by the head of every family.

Therefore, when the days of the Pasch came close—it was at the time of the full moon in spring—from all over the world Jews set out towards Jerusalem. The women were not obliged to go along, but the really pious women did, as we know from Anna, the mother of Samuel, who went every year. Children under twelve years were obviously not taken along. There was a two-fold coming of age for a Jewish boy. At twelve years he came of age before the law, and at twenty before the state. We in our countries are so used to the number twenty-one in connection with coming of age, that we have the feeling twelve is almost too soon. In the Orient, however, girls and boys mature so much earlier that a twelve-year-old boy there might be like an eighteen year old here. The Jews living in foreign countries, some many hundreds of miles away, were not bound to attend the Pasch every year in Jerusalem, but they wanted to come at least once in their lives. When they had come from such vast distances, they used to stay on for those fifty days until the Feast of Weeks, or Pentecost, and after that, return home. St. Luke tells us in the second chapter of the Acts of the Apostles about Pentecost: "Now there were dwelling at Jerusalem, Jews, devout men, out of every nation under Heaven." He continues to enumerate them, and it is very interesting to get hold of a map of the world as it was known at the time of Christ and find there "every nation under heaven."

There was a Jewish priest, Josephus Flavius by name, who lived just one generation after Our Lord, and who wrote down practically everything of interest about his time. His collected works have been brought out in a giant edition, and although some of it is tedious to read, he is still an almost inexhaustible source of information. He dwells at great length on those feasts and how they were celebrated. He is not always too accurate in numbers they say, and when he comes to talking about himself or his people, he is pretty much conceited, making a kind of wonder child out of himself. But otherwise we really learn things from him.

If we have made ourselves acquainted with the general picture of the countryside and this month of Nisan, as they called the early spring, when the land of Israel would be at its greenest and most beautiful and all the roads leading to Jerusalem would be swarming with pilgrims, then we pick out that one caravan, the one coming from Nazareth. Pilgrims hardly ever travel alone. Merely for safety's sake they prefer to travel in caravans. They also like the companionship, and as they ride on camels or donkeys or walk through the dust of the road, they chant psalms and hymns together and play on their flutes. In order to go from Galilee to Judea there were two main routes; we can find them on the map. The shortest one would lead through the country of Samaria. Samaria! The people living there were of mixed background, descending partly from the Hebrews and partly from the Gentiles who had been brought in by the kings of the Assyrians. In the Fourth Book of Kings 17:24, it says: "And the king of the Assyrians brought people from Babylon, and from Cutha, and from Avah, and from Emath, and from Sepharvaim: and placed them in the cities of Samaria. . . ." Because they were of mixed ancestry the Orthodox Jews hated them. To them they were heretics, and there was no worse epithet than to be called "thou Samaritan." One day the enraged Pharisees would hurl this name at Our Lord: "Thou art a Samaritan and hast a devil" (John 8:48). It sounds almost as if these two things belonged together. The Samaritans were shown this concept in most unmistakable terms. The Rabbis had compiled a whole code of laws and regulations as to how a Jew should behave with a Samaritan. He was allowed to look at him only once, just to make sure he was one. Then he had to avert his eyes and keep them averted. Of course, he was not allowed to touch him or touch anything which had been touched by a Samaritan—and so on and so on. So when we read about all these petty laws, we understand the surprise of the woman at Jacob's well when she says: "How dost thou, being a Jew, ask of me to drink, who am a Samaritan woman?" (John 4:9.) (It is really true: whatever we learn of the habits and customs will come in handy later when we lovingly study the Public Life of Our Lord.)

The pilgrims from Nazareth had to bring their own provisions for the pilgrimage. Nothing should be bought in Samaria. There were traditional overnight places all mapped out from of old. The first stop used to be made in Engannim. (In Josephus Flavius we would find it under the name Ginea, and on a modern map of our days, Jenim.) It is about two miles away from Nazareth, and the first village after the pilgrims were through the plains of Esdraelon. The Samaritans had a temple of their own on Mount Garizim, of which they were very jealous. Having rubbed in all the time what the Jews thought of them and their temple, didn't make the Samaritans any more friendly towards the Jews, and we learn of many hostilities breaking out in more or less bloody ways between them.

After the first night the pilgrims would go into the Samaritan hill country towards Sichem, which lay in a pass between the mountains. Here Father Abraham had once built an altar to the one true God. Father Jacob had given to his people the famous well; and Joseph, the most famous of his sons, was buried there. The second night was spent in famous Sichem. On the third day they had a twenty-five-mile stretch ahead of them to get to Beeroth. This was already out of the territory of the Samaritans. This was an insignificant little place only eight miles from Jerusalem, but it will never be forgotten because here it was that a mother discovered she had lost her Child. Tradition says that St. Helena and later the Crusaders built a church in memory of that sorrowful young mother who felt the sword pierce.

Thus on the last day the pilgrims had only eight miles more, and would arrive by noon in plenty of time to find shelter for the night.

All the tombs and sepulchres along the way would be freshly whitewashed so that they could be avoided by the pilgrims. Otherwise, if they should stumble over one, they would be liturgically unclean and not be able to celebrate the Pasch. Some day Our Lord will feel like calling somebody names, and will say to His adversaries: "You are like to white sepulchres . . ." (Matt. 23:27), which must be a crushing thing for an Orthodox Jew to be called.

And Jesus, Who, as a human Boy, could add new knowledge and progress in wisdom, was one of the pilgrims in that caravan in this memorable year. We can imagine how He, being of the highest intelligence, asked questions of His mother, with whom He would go to Jerusalem, all along the way, and how He would remember the holy history of His people throughout the ages. When they came into the hill country of Judea, the slopes would be simply covered with flocks of sheep. From Josephus Flavius we learn that once there were more than one hundred and twenty thousand lambs slaughtered in the temple at one Easter. As we know, every lamb had to be eaten by a group of people not less than ten nor more than twenty, so we can figure on an attendance of between two and three millions of pilgrims, and we can also figure for ourselves the size of the flocks of sheep. Now we can only guess what the Boy Jesus would think when He saw all those happy young lambs skipping about in the pastures. When we think that even the infused knowledge He had was much greater than that of all prophets and all angels together, so He must have known also in a human way what would happen to "the Lamb of God" twenty-one years hence.

On the next morning the pilgrims would catch their first glimpse of Jerusalem, the Holy City, and there, glittering with its golden roof—the temple—the temple! Beth Jahweh, it was called, the House of God. What must the Boy Jesus have felt when He saw the House of his Father for the first time. The Holy Family went into the Holy City by the Northern Gate.

The holy writers would remark on the handsomeness of young David and the wisdom of young Solomon. Here was more than David, here was more than Solomon—but no one seemed to notice a thing, and unrecognized, the Lord of heaven and earth came unto His own city and again, His own knew Him not.

Joseph would get busy procuring the paschal lamb, and knowing boys, it is more than likely that Jesus accompanied him. They had to find out also with whom they would join up to make a company of ten, to buy the bitter herbs and all that was needed for the celebration of the feast. All this had to be done before the end of the afternoon on the day before the feast.

When thinking back on the many folk customs we had in Austria, and how one responds as a child, with what eagerness one expects a certain day on which things will have to be done in a certain way again, it is most striking. This young Boy not only watched the preparations for the observance of the holy customs, He knew that all this was merely a symbol and He would be the fulfillment. With what eagerness did He watch!

And now we see them celebrate the feast. Every part of the ancient ceremony is described, the prayers which were uttered by Jesus, Mary and Joseph are written down. All we have to do is to look for it and tarry a little to add out of our own hearts the emotions which may have gone through those holiest of hearts. After all, their beloved Jesus would now be a Son of the law, no child any more. That is what singled out this Pasch from the others.

The Jews were not obliged to stay in Jerusalem for all the seven days of the Passover, but the really zealous ones did. Therefore, it must be the old Holy Week which St. Luke means when he says: "And having fulfilled the days, when they returned, the child Jesus remained in Jerusalem. And his parents knew it not" (Luke 2:43). When the pilgrims from Nazareth assembled at the Northern Gate, which was called the Damascus Gate, Jesus was not among them; but Mary must have thought: "Now as He is of age, He will be with Joseph and the men"; and Joseph might have thought: "He doesn't want to let His mother travel alone amid strangers; He must be with her." It must have been a most picturesque sight at this Damascus Gate because all the traffic going north, all the Galileans and the strangers from Trachonitis and Abilene, Damascus and as far as Antioch would organize into caravans there. As they left the gate, they would sing one of the psalms of the Hallel. Again it is something worth pondering when we think: just what must Mary and Joseph have been thinking about—and what had happened to Jesus? He may not have known until the very morning of this day when He

was ready to join His caravan that the Will of the Father
was otherwise. As we shall see later, the Will of the
Father was everything and all. "Because I came down from
heaven, not to do my own will but the will of him that sent
me" (John 6:38).

This is now a great mystery, why the Father retained
the Son in the temple. Did he want to give Him three days
of vacation, so to speak, and allow Him to dwell in His
presence as a human being in the closest way possible in
those days, in the temple? We don't know. We can only
ponder and wonder. We can want to know. We can ask the
Holy Ghost Who, as Our Lord promised, would some day
explain everything to us. Everything—what a word! Until
that day we just have to take it: the Father wished Jesus
to stay in the temple, and Jesus stayed without notifying
Mary and Joseph. This adds to the mystery. Why bring
all this anxiety on those good and most holy people, who
had done nothing all these years but try to be the best
possible keepers of the treasure entrusted to their care?
Until the Holy Ghost explains this better to us, we just
have to take what is written in Holy Scriptures: "For my
thoughts are not your thoughts: nor your ways my ways:
saith the Lord" (Isa. 55:8).

Then came that crucial evening when the caravan would
stop over again in Beeroth. That was arranged on purpose;
in case somebody had forgotten something or somebody
was left behind, it would not be too hard to catch up with
the caravan. And now comes the moment when Mary, who
hadn't seen her Boy for a full day, eagerly went over to find
Joseph and her Child. Joseph, on the other hand, was as
eager to see his family and be reunited with them for the
evening meal as was customary in those caravans where the
men and women traveled separately. Seeing each other,
the one question they must have asked simultaneously and
most anxiously was: "Where is Jesus?" and the horrified
answer, "I don't know. I thought He was with you." What
a terrible moment! The very next thing to do would be to
look all over the caravan, but nobody had seen Him. Nobody knew. The only conclusion therefore was that He

must have been left behind in Jerusalem. They would turn around immediately and go back.

Some books suggest that on the first day Mary and Joseph traveled as far as the overnight stop, and on the second day they traveled back to Jerusalem. I don't think so. How could they have closed an eye? How could they have waited an unnecessary minute? Years ago we were traveling in our big bus on a concert tour somewhere in New Hampshire, heading north. Some time in the afternoon I turned around from my seat and said: "Lorli, tell me, have you . . .?" and then I noticed that the seat where Lorli always sat was empty. I turned all the way around and got up and looked, and sure enough, she was not in the bus. Now eager talking and guessing started. The driver stopped. We had been driving for quite a number of hours with no rest. The last stop had been somewhere in Massachusetts, on the highway, to get a map of New Hampshire. Lorli was then a young child, maybe about as old as Jesus when He stayed behind in the temple. She must have slipped out unnoticed when we stopped at that gas station and now—where was she and what had happened to her meanwhile? All the stories of kidnapping and gangsters stood out in my mind and imagination can turn into your worst enemy at such times. Of course, we turned around, but none of us could really remember which gas station in that great countryside it had been. Of course, we called the police, but the State Police of New Hampshire couldn't do anything in Massachusetts, and we had to go back all the way. Finally we found her at the Police Headquarters listening in rapt attention to the stories of some of the highway policemen. Just from this little anecdote I know Mary and Joseph would turn around immediately. It was the time around full moon and the road would be light enough. This way back would be an ordeal when we think of all the caravans emerging towards the north, and Mary and Joseph worming their way through them. One very anxious thought must have troubled them most, the same thought which bothered us so much when we had turned around in the bus. Perhaps Lorli had gotten a ride in some car and we might miss her on the highway. So what if Jesus were amid the crowd constantly passing in the other direction? When they finally came to Jerusalem, having traveled sixteen miles, maybe not having eaten and in their anxiety not noticing that they had not, they must have been near collapse. The first place to go would be to their last night's lodgings. We don't know, however, whether they stayed with acquaintances or whether they camped in one of those innumerable white tents which were scattered all over the countryside outside the walls of Jerusalem. Then I am sure Mary and Joseph went straight to the temple. At this moment it will really come in handy that we have spent so much time on the temple previously, so that we know about those huge halls and stairways and galleries and cloisters, and we know that at this time about two hundred thousand people were milling around with all the noise of the Orient. Of course, they would ask the different members of the temple police whether they hadn't seen their Boy. Oh—they had seen so many boys, but they didn't remember *the* Boy. Now they must have gone out searching through the narrow streets for a whole day and a whole night, both weary to exhaustion. Joseph may have remembered another time when he saw Mary "drooping with fatigue"; and Mary felt the sword turning in her heart mercilessly. She hadn't had any warning. Never, never had Jesus caused them any anxiety or any trouble. Out of the blue sky had this cruel surprise come; and—was this the end? Would she never see Him again? Had He vanished out of their lives? Had He been kidnapped by some who had perhaps found out His identity or had He been kidnapped and sold as a slave like Joseph of old? Nothing had been revealed to her. She was not prepared, so her imagination must have run riot as that of every anxious mother in such a situation does. Where was He? What had happened to Him?

On the Sabbath and especially on high feasts the members of the Sanhedrin had established a custom of scattering throughout the temple and giving instructions on the scriptures to the people. They would seat themselves on a stool, the people at their feet. They would take a text of the Holy Books and start explaining it. After they had finished, there would always be a discussion. The people would eagerly ask questions and listen attentively to the answers, wisdom dropping from the lips of their venerated elders. In those days the Rabbis may have singled out a special Boy by the very questions He asked. They must have been delighted by the understanding this Youngster showed and by the beautiful manners He displayed, the modesty, humility, courtesy; and, in addition, the highest intelligence they had ever found among their own pupils. At the end of the first and second days the Rabbis, after having spent their time with the people, may have commented among themselves on this Boy; and on the third day they came together in a group enjoying the Boy. "And it came to pass that, after three days, they found him in the temple, sitting in the midst of the doctors, hearing them and asking them questions. And all that heard him were astonished at his wisdom and his answers" (Luke 2:46-47).

Again and again Mary and Joseph must have tried the temple, but the hour had not yet come, as it will be said several times in His life later. And He was concealed from their eyes in the throng and they did not see Him. On the third day, however, the Holy Ghost led their steps over to where Jesus was sitting in the midst of the teachers of Israel. When they saw Him so calm and so matter-of-course, the first thought which must have struck them must have been: "He has not been lost. He must have stayed behind knowing what He did." "And seeing him, they wondered." This we can well imagine. Wonder is not really the correct translation. It would rather be that they were awed and astonished. Never had they seen Him like this before: this new light in His eyes and a new dignity surrounding Him, which was somehow mirrored in the faces of the venerable old teachers, who treated Him almost as an equal. Mary and Joseph waited until they had finished and then His mother said to Him: "Son, why hast thou done so to us? Behold thy father and I have sought thee sorrowing."

Here we see Mary in a very special light. Later in His life it would happen to Our Lord that when His best friends got an inkling of Who He really was, they would somehow withdraw in awe and refuse to let Him humble Himself. So we see John the Baptist exclaim: "I ought to be baptized by thee, and comest thou to me" (Matt. 3:14). And when Our Lord was about to kneel down before Peter in order to wash his feet, Peter would refuse most excitedly: "Thou shalt never wash my feet" (John 13:8). And the Baptist and Peter had at that time only a fair idea of Who Jesus really was. Mary, however, knew it all the time. Humanly speaking, she must have felt from the very beginning like saying: "My Lord and My God, how could I ever act as authority over Thee? You must command me, not I You." It is always attributed to John's and Peter's humility that they acted the way they did; but we have to say that Mary's humility far outreached theirs. All these years she was obliged to accept services from her Child, Who also was her God, and to instruct Him and command Him. Now we see her even ask Him a question which sounds almost like a reproach. Every well-brought-up Jewish boy upon hearing this would get up and apologize humbly. Jesus did not, but answered: "How is it that you sought me? Did you not know that I must be about my father's business?" (Luke 2:49.) Again it is a pity that this translation has become popular, because it really should mean: "In My Father's House." From all the things which had happened in those heart-rending days, these words must have been the worst. "Did you not know?" Because they somehow implied that they should have known or could have known. Well—all we can say is: if Jesus Himself could grow in wisdom and grace before God and men, He Who was God at the same time, how much more is this true of Mary and Joseph who, after all, were only human. Both of them knew the secret mystery of this Child, but still they did not quite understand the word that he spoke to them. "The word" must have been this first manifestation of His being the Son of the Heavenly Father. With great tact Jesus at first does not contradict when Mary says:

"Behold thy father and I have sought thee sorrowing"; but then He immediately refers to God as His Father, the only one He would accept. As He was the Child in the family, Mary has a certain natural claim on Jesus—and Jesus does not deny it. Very soon He will prove how highly He regards that; but right now He has to inform them about His heavenly vocation. Later He will say one day: "He that loveth father or mother more than me is not worthy of me: and he that loveth son or daughter more than me is not worthy of me" (Matt. 10:37). "Amen I say to you, there is no man who hath left house or brethren or sisters or father or mother or children or lands, for my sake and for the gospel, who shall not receive an hundred times as much, now in this time; houses and brethren and sisters and mothers and children and lands, with persecutions: and in the world to come life everlasting" (Mark 10:29-30).

These were the first words spoken by Jesus as the Son of God and the Son of Man, which were written down in the Gospels. They seem almost like the title to His life story, because His whole life He will do nothing else but be about His Father's business.

Nineteen hundred years have passed since, and nobody has fully grasped the depths of these words, "Did you not know . . . ?" Mary and Joseph, St. Luke informs us, "understood not the word that he spoke unto them . . . And His mother kept all these words in her heart." A life full of pondering and contemplating on these and all His words will make Mary advance and grow to such an extent that never again will He have to say, "Did you not know . . .?"

XII

the carpenter

In the good old times when the craftsmen were the backbone of every country, and every village and every small town had its own blacksmith, tailor, shoemaker, tanner and, of course, carpenter, young boys between twelve and fourteen would be taken on as apprentices. They had to learn the craft from scratch. When an apprentice had learned how to handle all the tools, when he did not spoil anything any more, he advanced to the next stage, journeyman. That meant that he was working side by side with the master for a number of years until he was good enough to start his own work shop. Then he had to make his masterpiece, with which he showed all his skill. Unfortunately, our children will only know about these things through books, so fast are they dying out. This is the beginning of the end for every country. Coming from a country in Europe where the crafts are still at their height and good craftsmen greatly esteemed, we all missed them very much when we came to America. The first years in New York and Philadelphia were not so bad. We were used to the fact that in the elegant Kaerntnerstrasse in Vienna you didn't see craft shops with the master working in the window either. But when we moved up to northern New England, that's when we started worrying. We found out that the blacksmith in Stowe, who was a great artist in his craft, just couldn't find an apprentice; and the same thing has happened to Mr. Stafford the wonderful tinsmith, to Ben our town cobbler, and that's about all the crafts we have left. The young boys of this generation are not interested in learning a craft. Sometimes you find a rich boy who takes up a craft for a hobby; but that's not the right thing. He doesn't have to live from his handiwork, so he will not put his whole heart into it.

When the Son of God became man, what did He choose to be? A carpenter. Not as a hobby, but to make a living.

At first He was apprenticed to Joseph the carpenter. He started out by learning to use the tools, by doing little easy jobs, but mostly by watching the master. At sixteen or seventeen He was already working steadily with His foster father, being at least as good as he, if not better; because we can be sure that the Son of God made man was not only of the highly intelligence, filled with the greatest wisdom of mind and soul, but He also had the most skillful hands.

"And he went down with them and came to Nazareth and was subject to them. . . . And Jesus advanced in wisdom and age and grace with God and men" (Luke 2:51-52). Here we see this holiest, happiest family living in Nazareth; and are now setting out to explore the famous Hidden Life, which already is much less hidden to us because we know so much about His first twelve years. We see them get up at sunrise and go to sleep at sunset, a practice absolutely unknown to modern man. But oil and candles were expensive, and theirs was a life of frugality. We see the two men working either in the work shop or somewhere on a building according to the words of Genesis 3:19: "In the sweat of thy face shalt thou eat bread." St. Paul will later declare firmly: "If any man will not work, neither let him eat" (II Thess. 3:10). The Holy Family submitted fully to this plan of God. We see the woman of the house working all day long to do all her housework, heavy and light. She also had her craft, spinning and weaving. Tradition tells us that she was a master at it. The first centuries still admired the pieces of exquisite workmanship coming from her hands, as they also admired the farm implements and the pieces of furniture which had been made by Joseph the carpenter.

He "was subject unto them" is just another way of saying that He was obedient to Mary and Joseph, so we see Jesus grow up and when we want to find out what He did

in those long eighteen years in Nazareth, we finally see:
He prayed, He obeyed, and He worked; and not only He
alone, but all three of them. They prayed: we can find
their daily prayers, we can find out how they observed the
Day of the Lord. They must have recited the hymns,
prayers, and psalms contained in Holy Scriptures, and during many hours of their working day their thoughts dwelt
on the hidden meaning of what their lips had recited.
That's what they did when they were pondering. They
obeyed: "Behold the handmaid of the Lord; be it done to
me according to thy word" (Luke 1:38), and: "Did you not
know that I must be about my father's business?" (Luke
2:49.) These words uttered by Mary and Jesus give a deep
insight into their life of constant obedience to the Father.
From Joseph we know how promptly he reacted each time
an angel came. Theirs was a family life of obedience to the
Will of God. They worked, and we cannot dwell enough in
our thoughts on that fact that they worked; then the last
influence of those holy cards and statues of the Blessed
Mother in blue, St. Joseph in brown, and the Child or
Young Man in pink, all of them with a golden hem on
their garments and a dreamy look in their eyes, will be
destroyed. They worked like you and me and our neighbors on the left and right. This life of prayer, obedience,
and work created their strong mutual love, love of God
and love towards each other.

Books and books and books have been written on family
life. Our magazines and newspapers are full of alarming
articles on the danger of family life crumbling in our days.
Psychiatrists, psychoanalysts, and psychologists are busy
in research to answer the question "why." Little do they
seem to know that this question was answered two thousand years ago by a few words in the Gospel of St. Luke.
There we see the Heavenly Father making this tremendous
new foundation: the Christian family, when He sends His
Son into the small home in Nazareth. It is absolutely impossible to meditate too much on the Hidden Life. Just
watching Jesus, Mary, and Joseph in their daily routine

will do something for us. There is our model, and there is our only remedy. As the saying from the old country has it: If there are more mothers like Mary and more fathers like Joseph, there will be more children like Jesus.

XIII

the Son of Man

When later Jesus would come to the synagogue in Nazareth in order to preach there, the people would ask: "Is not this the carpenter, the son of Mary?" (Mark 6:3.) A son would only be spoken of in this way if the father was dead. Another time some relatives of Jesus wanted to bring Him home. They would never have interfered if the father of the house had been living. And when Our Lord gave His mother into the care of John, His disciple, then it is definitely sure that Joseph, her husband, was dead. Through tradition we learn that Joseph died when Jesus was eighteen years old. If this is really true, then Jesus and Mary must have gotten a legal guardian, usually one of the relatives, to take care of their affairs until the Son would be twenty years old.

There have always been references to the happiness of St. Joseph's death because he died in the presence of Jesus and Mary. When we think that Jesus would later break out in tears and cry at His friend's tomb—how much more will He have shown His grief when His foster father died, he who was so much nearer and dearer to Him than Lazarus. When the dying Joseph saw the tears in the eyes of his Lord and God and understood that they were shed for him—we can understand that his was a happy death.

Now it was even more quiet in the little house where a widow lived with her only Son. When Jesus was twenty years old, He became of age before the state. He took over officially the responsibility and care of His mother, and He was now the heir to all of Joseph's possessions. From now on He was the Master of the house: Until then He had been "subject unto them." From now on when a question was to be decided, Mary would bring it to Jesus and He would decide.

Many mysteries are contained in these next ten years when Jesus and Mary lived so close together. Outwardly we can reconstruct to a great extent their simple and uncomplicated life, but what must it have been in their souls?

To understand even the slightest little bit about Mary, we shall have to go back to paradise when God had created men according to His image and likeness. We would have to meditate at length on what Adam and Eve were like before the fall. How much do we know about how life was in the State of Grace, when men could converse with God like children with their Father, when they used to walk with Him in the garden every day at the evening breeze? There is a great deal to be found out by meditating on mankind before and after sin. It is exasperating how little we know of things which we could know, only because we don't think about them. The worst part of this our ignorance is that we don't even know how ignorant we are. Mary and Jesus belonging to the creation before sin were like Adam and Eve only infinitely more so, and they were placed in a world dark with sin. What must it have meant to these two people in the world who alone were full of grace? We shall never really find out in this life, but it is very much worth while to begin to try.

It must have been a mystery to Mary that her Son, Whom she knew to be the Messiah, went right on as a carpenter now He was twenty-five, twenty-eight, twenty-nine years old. But in her State of Grace she knew no curiosity. She may not even have asked Him what He planned to do.

How must it have been for Him? As Man on His early pilgrimages to Jerusalem He saw His Father's House made into a den of thieves. He was just as outraged about it in His innermost soul when He was twenty-five or twenty-nine as later when at thirty He would take a little scourge or ropes. There we learn something of His long-suffering patience in waiting for His hour to come.

Whatever we know about St. John of the Cross, St. Teresa of Avila, and other great mystics, what they tell us of their insight into divine things—Mary and Jesus from their first moment on possessed more of this insight than all the mystics put together. Without the necessity of speaking a word, their souls were closely united in God.

a word in between

Usually books have only forewards or introductions. I have come to a spot in this book now where I want very badly to explain something about what is to come. First I had it in the foreward, which I shrewdly called "how it happened," just in case there are other people like me who always skip forewards. But it didn't really fit in that place. I couldn't possibly say it in the text either, so please allow me to say "a word in between."

This book really does not want to become a "Life of Christ." It only wants to serve as a stimulus to all families to reconstruct their own "Life of Christ," parents and children together, simply by telling what we did.

One of the reasons why it is so wonderful to search through the life of Christ as a family is that children always ask questions and expect answers, honest answers. And if you say: "I really don't know," they will ask: "Couldn't you find out?"

After having finished reading "Yesterday," you might have one big question on your mind: "But where in the world did you find all this information, all these many details of the Childhood Story of Our Lord, which only takes a few pages in my New Testament?"

There I must answer: aren't we lucky, and by "we" I mean all people of our days. A generation or two ago all the precious knowledge about the circumstances of the land and times of Christ politically, socially, and spiritually, as well as the findings of archaeologists, were hidden away in great scholarly works, some of them written in Latin, Greek, or Hebrew. They were locked up in professional libraries, inaccessible to the common man. Within our own generation, however, there have appeared on the market a number of most helpful books. Scholars have dedicated a whole lifetime to compiling this information and giving it to us in readable English. There are Gospel commentaries like: *Jesus Christ* by Léonce de Grandmaison, S. J.; *The Gospel of Jesus Christ* by M. J. LaGrange, O. P. (Newman Press); *The Public Life of Our Lord Jesus Christ* by Archbishop Goodier; *The Life of Our Lord* by Moritz Meschler, S. J. (Herder); *Life of Jesus* by François Mauriac (David McKay Co., Inc.); *Life of Christ* by J. Papini (Harcourt, Brace and Company); *Life of Christ* by Ricciotti; *Jesus Christ, His Life, His Teaching, and His Work* by Ferdinand Prat, S. J.; *Mary the Mother of Jesus* by F. M. William (Herder); then the two precious books by Father Denis O'Shea, *Mary and Joseph, Their Life and Times* and *The Holy Family*. Every home should also have a Bible encyclopedia in one volume with many illustrations. There you can look up anything you want to know about agriculture, flowers, herbs, trees, animals, wearing apparel, arts and crafts, business transactions, villages, towns, and cities, homes, nutrition, and worship.

In the summer we conduct a camp. It is a Music Camp, and it lies at the foot of the hill where we live. There we conduct four Sing Weeks every year, each of which is ten days long. The third one is always a Liturgical Sing Week, dealing with church music and questions of the liturgy, and for this Sing Week there are usually quite a number of priests, seminarians, and sisters. A number of wonderful friendships have been formed through the camp, and these friends return to us whenever they can come, even if the camp is not open. Then they come to our house, and there in the living room is the famous bay window, famous for the most interesting and wonderful discussions we have had there with them. The remarkable thing has happened, and still does: whatever the problem under discussion may be, it will invariably lead to taking our copies of the New Testament and searching through its pages for the answer which, of this we are dead sure, it must contain.

By the way: this word, problem, has only slipped in here. It should really be eliminated from the vocabulary of a Christian. When we look at the first Christian era, we see there were no problems. If something came their way in the line of adversities, they treated it first as an obstacle. An obstacle we have to overcome. We have to do everything in our power to get rid of it. Only after we have tried everything and it still doesn't move, then we know. This is not an obstacle, this is a cross. If obstacles are meant to be overcome, crosses are meant to be borne, and if we can manage at all, borne gladly according to His example. "Problems" are a dangerous hybrid of modern times. They seem to be meant only and solely to be talked about. How often you find when you earnestly try to help somebody with his problems, how often you learn to your own astonishment that he doesn't really want that. He needs problems in order to be able to talk about himself. This is a disease of our time. Just watch little children; they never have problems. They may have obstacles to encounter, and no one is as persistent as a little child in trying to overcome an obstacle! They may have, small as they are, a cross to carry, and it is very touching to watch how patiently children suffer. But in their life is no room for a problem. They are not yet busy with themselves. Then we have Our Lord. He most certainly had obstacles to overcome, and He did it with flying colors. As long as it was the time to fight: whether it was the Pharisees or at times His own slow-witted disciples or His own tiredness, or Satan with all his pomps and all his works, He shows us how to fight obstacles. And when the time has come when the Father sends Him the cross, He most certainly shows what to do with a cross. But in His whole life there is no problem. We shall be astonished when we notice how often the word creeps into our conversation, but we should consciously fight it.

We in the family have done it now quite often, starting at the beginning and going with Him through His life as much as possible day by day, first thirty times three hundred sixty-five days, most of them spent in Nazareth; and

then watching how He leaves His peaceful home because
the Father is calling: the time is fulfilled—His hour has
come. Now come the last thousand days of His life. After
we have watched Him and listened to Him in the most
varied situations, one word finally sticks in our minds,
when He says at the end: "For I have given you an example, that as I have done to you, so you do also" (John
13:15). From then on only one thing matters in our life:
to find out what Jesus would do, how He would react, what
He would say in our stead as we go from day to day.

While sitting in the bay window, usually having a cup of
coffee right after lunch or right after supper, all kinds of
difficulties will come up for discussion. Very often a startled,
perplexed silence will follow when we are confronted with
the question: What would Our Lord do in such a case?
The thing to do then is for everyone to take his own copy
of the New Testament and, sitting around the octagonal
table with the coffee, one has to thumb through the pages
and look for something which fits the situation. Isn't it
glorious and almost incredible that we have *never* looked
in vain? This frequent thumbing through the Gospels—
besides bringing the answers to our questions—has another
wonderful effect, and a two-fold one. Not only do we really
find our way around the Gospels very soon and know that
this comes only in Luke, whereas that only John talks
about, and something else can only be found in Matthew
or Mark; but we also learn to know Him better and better.
Now it is not so much His times and their customs that we
are getting to know; now it is His own character. More and
more we are overwhelmed by what we find. It is heartwarming.

TWO

TODAY

XIV

"the other cheek"

It was pouring outside. The Worcester Range beyond
Stowe Hollow couldn't even be seen, it was so foggy. Such
weather invites one to prolong one of those coffee sessions.
In the bay window were four priests, a few seminarians,
and some of us. Maria was "boring."

(This is a family joke which goes back to our first year
in America. After a concert we were invited to a reception
in somebody's house, and obviously as a special lure to us,
it was said that Mrs. So-and-so was pouring. Our Martina,
very young then and always known for her rather careless
diction, said to our aghast hostess:

"What does it mean that Mrs. So-and-so is boring?"

It traveled fast from lady to lady and was the joke of
the evening because it so happened, the hostess told us under her breath, that Mrs. So-and-so *was* boring!

That has stuck with us ever since, and whenever the coffee pot is brought in, somebody raises the question: "And
who is boring today?")

"I have such difficulties with 'the other cheek,' " began
Father O'Shaughnessy. "I just can't understand it. It
doesn't seem right to me. It doesn't seem manly. If someone strikes me on the right cheek, does it mean that I
should really and truly turn the other one also, or if someone steals my coat, that I should run after him and offer
him my suit also? I just don't get it."

"Doesn't that serve as an introduction to 'But I say to
you, love your enemies'?" said Father Di Silva.

"Let's get our New Testaments," I suggested. That was
a nice little break. Everyone had to get up to get his copy,

and meanwhile we could do a little thinking. Sure, there we found it in Matthew 5:38-48:

"You have heard that it hath been said, An eye for an eye, and a tooth for a tooth. But I say to you not to resist evil: but if one strike thee on thy right cheek, turn to him also the other: And if a man will contend with thee in judgment, and take away thy coat, let go thy cloak also unto him. And whosoever will force thee one mile, go with him the other two. Give to him that asketh of thee, and from him that would borrow of thee turn not away. You have heard that it hath been said, Thou shalt love thy neighbor, and hate thy enemy. But I say to you, Love your enemies: do good to them that hate you: and pray for them that persecute and calumniate you: That you may be the children of your Father who is in heaven, who maketh his sun to rise upon the good, and bad, and raineth upon the just and the unjust. For if you love them that love you, what reward shall you have? do not even the publicans this? And if you salute your brethren only, what do you more? do not also the heathens this? Be you therefore perfect, as also your heavenly Father is perfect."

"Before we get into any arguments, let's look now what Our Lord Himself did with these words in His own life," began our Father Wasner. "Let's turn the pages and stop wherever we find something under the heading: Our Lord and His enemies."

We started reading, and whoever found something, read it aloud. One of us had paper and pencil to write down the place and something like a resumé of the quotation. In about two hours we had gone through the four Gospels and had found about ninety places where Our Lord is either dealing with His enemies or discussing the subject with His disciples. Now we took those different passages, read them, tried to compare them, and all of a sudden something occurred to us. Whenever Our Lord meets enemies who are His very own personal enemies, He always reacts with meekness and humility, and with so much patience. For instance, the first enemy in His life was Herod, who wanted to destroy Him. Meekly and humbly

He flees from him. We always have to keep in mind that His was not the case of the ordinary refugee who hasn't much choice, but has to flee. At any moment Our Lord could have defended Himself, as He says so unmistakably to His disciples in Gethsemane: "Thinkest thou that I cannot ask my Father, and he will give me presently more than twelve legions of angels?" (Matt. 26:53.) If we keep this always before our mind—what He could have done to His enemies—only then are we duly impressed in watching what He actually does. Any number of times the Scribes or Pharisees want to catch Him with a tricky question. He knows that. For the longest time, instead of giving way to His righteous indignation, He will stand them, answering their questions quietly but with a divine thoroughness as if pleading with them: "Don't you see how wrong you are?" After a few years of this method, the disciples seem to have had enough of it, seeing that the adversaries were only getting fresher and didn't seem to be converted through His patience. They want to show the Pharisees their place by force. Take the time when He wanted to enter a Samaritan town and the Samaritans did not allow Him. When James and John the Apostles saw this, they were outraged. "Lord," they cried, "wilt thou that we command fire to come down from heaven and consume them?" But no, that was not what He wanted. "You know not of what spirit you are," He said gently. "The Son of man came not to destroy souls, but to save" (Luke 9:54-56). We see Him go through His last days fearless, uncompromising with His enemies, but always with an outstretched hand. He could not have shown this in a more touching way than when the traitor finally catches Him in the garden and Jesus says imploringly: "Friend, whereto art thou come?" (Matt. 26:50.) Just a few short hours ago He had warned this man. This is now the fullness of "turning the other cheek" when He says to Judas, "Friend." On the cross He will sum up His whole attitude towards His personal enemies, His willingness to forgive and forget: "Father, forgive them, for they know not what they do" (Luke 23:34). "And if a man will contend with thee in judgment

and take away thy coat, let go thy cloak also unto him"
(Matt. 5:40), He had said before. Now on the cross they
have not only taken His coat, they have taken all, so they
think, even His life. And after His death He will give still
a little more than they have taken. A lance will open His
Heart, the last drop of His blood He will give. In such
greatness do we see Him live His own words.

But then there is another element in meeting enemies if
they are not His own private, personal antagonists, if they
happen to be enemies of the Father, doing wrong towards
Him Who has sent Our Lord. Then we see Him as very
different. "And when he had made, as it were, a scourge
of little cords, he drove them all out of the temple. . . .
Take these things hence, and make not the house of my
Father a house of traffic" (John 2:15-16). He shouts at
them. When the Pharisees and scribes have had sufficient
time, when He has pleaded long enough with them, showing them by miracles that He really is "the One," and
when there is no more doubt that they simply don't want
to believe, then they turn from being His private enemies
into being the enemies of God. They have rejected His
divine grace, and they are responsible that others might
miss it, too. There we see Our Lord in anger and wrath.
One can almost see His lips tremble and hear His voice
shout when He addressed them: "Blind guides, who strain
out a gnat and swallow a camel. . . . Woe to you, scribes
and Pharisees, hypocrites; because you are like to whited
sepulchres, which outwardly appear to men beautiful but
within are full of dead men's bones and of all filthiness.
. . . You serpents, generation of vipers, how will you flee
from the judgment of hell?" (Matt. 23:24, 27, 33).

"That brings home a point to me," said Father Jackson,
a wonderful elderly priest, "and it gets stronger by the
minute as I look at these verses. Don't we usually react
in just the opposite way to Our Lord's way? When anyone
shows up as His personal enemy, He is meek and humble
and practically takes the person on His lap; but when it
comes to the honor of God, then He speaks His mind
fearlessly, and never mind what might happen to Him

afterwards. And we? How often does it happen that in our company things are said which are definitely against God or His Church or His commandments, and if we can manage at all, we turn a deaf ear so as not to get into an embarrassing situation; but woe if anyone steps on our own toes! Then we are up in arms. Am I right?''

At this moment the bell rang. What could that mean? I was stupefied myself, because the bell usually rings only for meals. But there—looking at my watch, I saw it was time for supper. Heavens! I didn't want to say it right there and then, but it has happened before that while we were engaged in such conversations, the hours have passed like minutes.

As the dinner bell had interrupted us in the middle of a sentence, the conversation went right on during supper. And when we sat once more around the coffee in the bay window afterwards, Father O'Shaughnessy asked the momentous question: "But just how does one do it? I do understand now what 'turning the other cheek' really means, but in practical everyday life—how do I love my enemy?''

Between three of us—each one sounded as if he would know what he was talking about—we tried to answer this question.

You many very well have lived a long life saying the Our Father daily and when you came to the words, "and forgive us our trepasses as we forgive those who trespass against us,'' your soul was completely quiet and unruffled. Then one day something happens. It may all be your own fault. You may have a bad argument and the other one walks out on you bitter and full of wrath. Before you can think twice, you have an enemy. At first, you don't want to believe it. You say to yourself, he'll come around, just wait a little. But this happens to be one of those unfortunate cases where he does not come around. After awhile you may say that's perfectly ridiculous, and you may earnestly try to meet him, and in a casual way get things straightened out. But then, you find out that he's fed up with you and he has no intention whatsoever of having things as they were. Soon you will hear how he spoke about you on this or that occasion, and from those remarks you know now that you have an enemy.

Soon after this startling discovery, these words emerge from the depths of your memory and they take on a completely new meaning: "You have heard that it hath been said, Thou shalt love thy neighbor and hate thy enemy. But I say to you, Love your enemies" (Matt. 5:43-44).

And now, a new period in your life begins: You try, you really try, to love your enemy; but how? There have been a number of different loves in your life and these you try to apply now to him. How you loved your parents when you were very young yourself—how you loved your best friend in school—how you loved in those unique weeks before your wedding—how you now love your own children. Then there is in your heart love for your country, for your home town, for your home, for your old school and your neighborhood—it is perfectly amazing how many shades of love move a human heart during one short life. But, as hard as you may try—not one of them fits your purpose. Now, you almost get worried because there is that command: "But I say to you. . . .," and you haven't yet found a way to fulfill it. This much you have learned, however, that the love for your enemy is a completely new love in your life and you have to discover it step by step.

All you are doing now is *wanting* to love your enemy. As you want to love him, you are getting very much concerned about him, and this is the first step. You realize that he really shouldn't be your enemy—nobody really should stubbornly resist reconciliation—and with an anxious heart you realize that it cannot do him much good.

As the natural outcome of this, your concern, you find yourself talking with God about your enemy. This is the second step. You say: "Dear Lord, please don't take this too seriously; I really don't think he means it quite the way it sounds. Don't forget how much I antagonized him, and please, dear Lord, I want you to know there is no bitterness in my heart against him whatever he might say or do." There's a great urge in your heart to make sure about this because you realize that *if* you'd get angry and bitter and have your own spiritual life badly influenced by all this, it would be partly his fault and he would be held responsible.

As time goes on, you discover that there is a change taking place in yourself. Since that person of whom you thought so highly, who was so close to you, and to whom you were so much attached has turned against you, you find that you get more and more detached from other people, because you are aware that what happened once could happen any day again. And there you find that your enemy has done you a great service, and most eagerly you point that out in your next talks with God. This is the third step. However, even if it has helped you, it should not continue. You would not want to die or want him to die, still your enemy. Now you begin to storm heaven. "The return of the brother" becomes your foremost intention. You ask all your friends to help you pray for a "certain intention." And whatever comes your way in the line of suffering is greeted with a smile, be it physical pain or mental anguish, because it can be used to be offered up for the most important person in your life, your enemy. This is the last step.

Now you have found the love for your enemy. It is completely different from all other loves, and it is very anxious and very unemotional. It resides mostly in your will, but let up hope that in the eyes of God it is a soaring fire which, in His own good time, will melt all the ice or resistance. And Our Lord's wish will be fulfilled: "That they may be one . . . that they may be made perfect in one" (John 17:22-23).

XV

"I have called you friends"

The next day was one of those beautiful days which make every visitor exclaim at the view from our mountaintop. They have never seen anything like it. We wanted to make up to our friends who had been sitting indoors for quite some time, and we took them across the valley to the opposite mountain range up to the Stowe Pinnacle. After a stiff climb of about two hours we emerged out of the woods onto that huge round rock which crowns the Pinnacle like a cupola. There we feasted our eyes on a three-hundred-sixty-degree view. Then we had a picnic lunch.

Father Jones said: "I could hardly get to sleep last night. I kept on thinking about our discussion. I wonder, could we do it once more and find out something about Our Lord and His friends?"

"I don't think right now, Father," I said, "because we would need our New Testaments."

Lo and behold, out of coat pockets, vest pockets, and knapsacks appeared little books. Everybody had brought his New Testament—except me. Was this a conspiracy? No—everybody had just "hoped we would do it again."

"I can truthfully say," said Father Jackson, pipe dangling, "that I have read and meditated a great deal on the Scriptures in my life, but I have never felt as good as yesterday with all of us working on one topic. Light just seemed to stream out of the lines. Did anybody else feel like that?"

Looking around, he met only with eager nods. I knew so well what he meant, from our family sessions. After all, Our Lord had once said: "For where there are two or three gathered together in my name, there am I in the midst of them" (Matt. 18:20). In earlier years when the children were small, we used to have an empty chair for Our Lord, Who had promised to be in our midst. This is an altogether different presence from the omnipresence of God or the Eucharistic Presence in the Blesses Sacrament. It is a very real presence, however, and one can always feel something of the sensation of the two disciples walking to Emmaus as they expressed it afterwards: "Was not our heart burning within us, whilst he spoke in the way and opened to us the scriptures?" (Luke 24:32.)

We sat in a circle, and someone remarked: "This is almost as good as in the bay window."

"Except for the coffee," said Father Jackson swinging his pipe.

Soon we were deeply involved in turning pages, watching Jesus with His friends. All of us will remember this afternoon when we took such a deep look into the Heart of a Friend.

There were first of all the twelve men He had picked out of the crowd. They were chosen by Himself. They didn't know it at the beginning, but they were meant to be His friends. One day He will say so clearly and unmistakably to them: "I will not now call you servants. . . . But I have called you friends" (John 15:15). As we turn the pages of the Gospels, we see Him deal with them. According to tradition, Thomas and Judas were a little more educated, but the others seem to have been fishermen except for one, who was a tax collector. And He was the Son of God! What a time He had opening their minds to His revolutionary ideas; stopping them from being materialistic, from grabbing immediate reward; getting them out of their smallish provincialism with its "What will people say?" into the world-wide outlook of "Go and teach *all* nations," and "And I say to you my friends: Be not afraid of them who kill the body and after that have no more that they can do" (Luke 12:4). Sometimes He gets really exasperated when they don't seem to get the point. "O unbelieving and perverse generation, how long shall I be with you? How long shall I suffer you?" (Matt. 17:16.)

With their boats and nets they were certainly used to a hard life. They soon found out, however, that when they gave up everything they had been doing so far in order to follow Him, they were just going from one kind of hard work to another. Their Lord and Master, as they called Him at that time, was Himself the most hard-working Man they had ever met, day and night, seven days a week, four weeks a month—whenever anybody needed Him. Isn't it somewhat significant that they said: "Lord, teach us to pray" (Luke 11:1), but never, "Lord, teach us to work." There were no days off, and unending hours of work. He never set up headquarters with an office and office hours in Jerusalem or Capharnaum, where the people could have come to see Him. He was always on the go after the lost sheep. What vast distances He would cover, either in tropical heat or torrential rains! And what He did, He expected of His friends. Peter remembers it after thirty long years: often they were so rushed they didn't even have time to eat!

At the same time, Jesus noticed what was going on, and once we see Him taking a rest. They had just gotten the news that John the Baptist had been killed. Our Lord's Heart was then so filled with sympathy towards His friends (some of whom had first been disciples of John), that He said: "Come apart . . . and rest a little" (Mark 6:31). How gratefully must they have crowded into Peter's boat and taken a picnic lunch along and begun to row over the lake expecting a quiet weekend. But the crowd had outwitted them. The people saw what was going on, ran along the shore, and arrived before the boat. Immediately Our Lord forgot His own exhaustion and began to talk to the people, and of course, He expected the same of His friends. Finally He even told them to feed that big crowd (about five thousand). All we know from the Gospel is that the twelve had to minister to the people, distribute bread and fish until everyone was satisfied. We don't hear a word about what happened to them. Maybe when all their guests were happily gone, they could eat from the leftovers in the twelve baskets.

One of the toughest lessons for them must have been to

realize that the time when they were in a safe business where one could calculate how much one would make and how one could build up for the future, was gone. We can see how worried they were about this fact when Peter asked Our Lord outright just how much they were going to make for themselves. The answer was not encouraging. He was promised an ample reward after death. But they would not give up. Time and again they would come up with such questions. Two of them would even get their mother to make a petition, but then as before, it doesn't get them anywhere. "Even as the Son of man is not come to be ministered unto, but to minister" (Matt. 20:28). "The disciple is not above the master" (Matt. 10:24). All right. They had swallowed to some little extent this bitter pill. But couldn't the ministering be restricted to nice people? Never mind the poor and the sick, but outcasts like tax collectors, bad women, Samaritans! Was it really necessary for a respectable, honorable man to mix with them? Obviously it was. And it didn't stop with talking to them, either. They had to learn to eat with them and learn from their Master, uncomfortable though they must have felt about it, how one can even understand and finally like and defend them. It must have been one of the minor shocks when they heard Him say: "Amen I say to you that the publicans and the harlots shall go into the kingdom of God before you" (Matt. 21:31). Sometimes there seemed to be nothing refined about His taste. All this time, however, their love for Him grew. So when Our Lord would say on that fatal morning when many of the "nice" people turned their backs on Him: "Will you also go away?" Peter could answer in the name of all: "Lord, to whom shall we go? Thou hast the words of eternal life" (John 6:68-69). The great love and patience He had lavished on them were bearing fruit.

They must have been courageous men if they had worked on the Sea of Galilee. This big lake is famous and feared for the sudden squalls which arise. The people say that Lake Champlain, which is not very far from us in Stowe, has an ugly temper. That's what people felt towards the Sea of Galilee. Now these men had to learn a new kind of courage. "Behold we go up to Jerusalem," He would say to them one day, "and all things shall be accomplished . . ." (Luke 18:31). And knowing all these dangers now, they still had to go. They were constantly mixed up with the priests and Pharisees, whom their Master almost seemed to provoke. One almost sees them wince when He had to cure somebody again on the Sabbath, knowing already the inevitable outcome.

With all His great love and endless patience, and in spite of their slow-growing understanding, once in a while He had to scold them. For instance, when they one day didn't want mothers to bring their children to Him; or the crushing retort when Peter, meaning so well, advised Him to stay away from Jerusalem.

And all the while they didn't have a steady income. They lived on alms. They had no income. They were worse off than the fox who had his den and the birds who had their nests—they had no security. And still we never hear them really complain. Sometimes they quarrel among themselves, not infrequently they behave stupidly, but they always appreciate that what He is asking of them is not even a small particle of what He demands of Himself.

Here I looked up and met Hester's eyes smiling at me.

"Where is it, Hester?" I said.

"At home in the file 'Mother Private,' " she answered, "but I know it. Do you want to hear it?"

And Hester, having recently typed up that little poem of which we spoke now because we thought it so nicely fitting, recited:

"REPARTEE

by Alfred Barrett (1906–   )

"Because her bucking cart-mule
    Showed scant respect for a saint,
There rose from a ditch near *Medina*
    Del Campo this complaint.

" 'Why do you treat me thus, dear Lord?
    I'd willingly shed my blood,

But I balk at the prospect of martyrdom
  In this Castilian mud!'

"Smiled Christ—'Thus do I treat My friends,
  So must I thus treat you . . .'
'No wonder, Lord,' sighed Teresa,
  'No wonder You have so few.' "[1]

Everybody laughed except Peter. He didn't even listen, but stared fascinatedly into his New Testament. Peter had been a Navy officer in the war, and he is our second oldest friend in America. The Navy always finds the Navy, and so he had become a special friend of my husband. We will never forget how we met him. It was on a day in September, a really unpleasant, wet, foggy, cold New England autumn day. It was our first summer in Stowe on the farm where the old house had fallen in and we camped in tents and barns doing as much work on the farm as we possibly could. On this day we had just finished digging the potatoes out and were now sorting them in a shed when a young Navy officer climbed up our hill, clad in immaculate white, bringing greetings from Michael, a mutual friend. After the exchange of the first few polite phrases the incautious young man said: "Is there anything I could do to help?" Off he went in overalls to the potatoes.

For years to come we would have to listen to his funny descriptions of his aching back. Having a wonderful sense of humor, he very soon became famous for his story-telling. When the war was over and Peter wanted to go back into his former business, he met Our Lord, Who said: "Come, follow Me." Unlike the rich young man, he sold everything he had and went and followed Him; and so the elegant young Navy officer was now a seminarian. As he looked up from his book, there was a different expression on his face. His usually laughing eyes had a new and almost tender light.

"Please look up St. John," he said, "beginning with the thirteenth chapter. If we have found out so far what He

[1] From *Mint by Night*, published by America Press, 1938.

did with His friends, here we seem to learn how He really felt about them.''

We looked and—Peter was right. What a different language! One almost wonders whether this is the same Person Who had exclaimed a few pages before: "How long shall I suffer you," when He says now:

"Little children, yet a little while I am with you. . . .

"Let not your heart be troubled. You believe in God; believe also in me. . . .

"If you shall ask me any thing in my name, that I will do. If you love me, keep my commandments. . . .

"I will not leave you orphans, I will come to you. . . .

"He that hath my commandments, and keepeth them; he it is that loveth me. And he that loveth me, shall be loved of my Father and I will love him, and will manifest myself to him. . . .

"If any one love me, he will keep my word, and my Father will love him, and we will come to him, and will make our abode with him. . . .

"These things have I spoken to you, abiding with you. But the Paraclete, the Holy Ghost, whom the Father will send in my name, he will teach you all things, and bring all things to your mind, whatsoever I shall have said to you. Peace I leave with you, my peace I give unto you. . . .

"Let not your heart be troubled, nor let it be afraid. . . .

"As the Father hath loved me, I also have loved you. Abide in my love. If you keep my commandments, you shall abide in my love, as I also have kept my Father's commandments and do abide in his love.

"These things I have spoken to you, that my joy may be in you, and your joy may be filled. This is my commandment, that you love one another, as I have loved you. Greater love than this no man hath, that a man lay down his life for his friends. You are my friends, if you do the things that I command you. I will not now call you servants, for the servant knoweth not what his lord doth. But I have called you friends because all things whatsoever I have heard of my Father, I have made known to you. . . .

"In the world you shall have distress, but have confidence, I have overcome the world. . . ."

We had long stopped looking at our books but were listening to Peter's ringing voice solemnly reading this story of the greatest friendship the world has ever seen. But the greatest was still to come when Our Lord, after having opened His Heart to His friends, raising His eyes to heaven, said to His Father:

"I have manifested thy name to the men whom thou hast given me. . . . Thine they were, and to me thou gavest them, and they have kept thy word. Now they have known, that all things which thou hast given me are from thee because the words which thou gavest me I have given to them. . . . And they have believed that thou didst send me.

"I pray for them. I pray not for the world, but for them whom thou hast given me. . . .

"And not for them only do I pray, but for them also who through their word shall believe in me, that they also may be one, as thou, Father, in me, and I in thee. . . .

"Father, I will that where I am, they also whom thou hast given me may be with me. . . .

A deep and long silence followed. It was not uncomfortable, it was rather a happy and satisfied silence. As we looked down on the treetops at our feet far out into the valley over to Mount Mansfield or, lying on our backs, up into the deep blue sky, the one word started working in our hearts: "And not for them only do I pray, but for them also who through their word shall believe in me." And with deep gratitude in our hearts, we understood that this meant us.

An indescribable happiness wells up in the heart when one realizes that this is the way He talks about His friends to the Father, even if He forsees that soon they will be scattered in their houses and leave Him alone. Thus enveloped and protected, the feeling of greatest peace—modern man calls it security—settles in the soul. With great eagerness one wishes, however, to make absolutely sure that one belongs to this inner circle. That's why it is so good to know that He said: "You are my friends, if you do the things I command you." And a moment later: "These things I command you, that you love one another."

XVI

"He . . . healed them"

Once again we were sitting in the bay window with another family, very close friends of ours; Paul and Mary and their three oldest children, and Father Wasner. Paul is a doctor, and the conversation turned towards miracles.

"Not so long ago," said Mary, "we had five doctors and their wives for dinner. On that evening we had a lively discussion of miracles. Paul and I have wanted ever since to look up all the miracles of Our Lord, but we haven't gotten around to it. Would it perhaps be possible. . . . ?"

In a short time we were busy turning pages again, Mary listing the headlines:

> The wedding of Cana
> Cure of the official's son
> Exorcism of a demoniac
> Peter's mother-in-law
> The draught of fishes
> Cure of a leper
> Cure of a paralytic
> Cure of a withered hand
> "Lord, I am not worthy. . . ."
> The widow of Naim
> The storm on the lake
> Geraza
> The daughter of Jairus
> The woman with the hemorrhage
> Cure of two blind and one mute
> The pool of Bethsaida
> Feeding of five thousand

Feeding of four thousand
Walking on the water
The Syro-Phoenician woman
Cure of the deaf-mute
Cure of the blind
The Transfiguration
Cure of the lunatic boy
The money in the mouth of the fish
The man born blind
The paralytic in Capharnaum
The stooped woman
The man with the dropsy
The ten lepers
Lazarus
His own Resurrection
Mass cures: "... He ... healed them."

Every one of those stories had been read aloud. Now we looked at the list, and quite naturally, miracles seemed to group themselves: There were cures; there were exorcisms; there were miracles of nature, like the storm on the lake and His walking on the water; there were miracles of a completely supernatural character like the happenings at Jesus' Baptism, the Transfiguration, and the Resurrection.

One of the youngsters suggested that we write the headlines of each one on a little card so that we could group them on the table. We did.

The large group of cures was subdivided very soon into cures which happened through touching and others which took place through a mere act of His will. We found that while "He, laying his hands on every one of them, healed them" (Luke 4:40), He never touches one possessed by a devil. He only rebukes the devils. Sometimes He says to the suffering ones: "Go," and the miracle happens after their departure. Once He says to an official whose son was sick in another town, "Go thy way; thy son liveth" (John 4:50). Another time He goes into quite a long ceremony with the deaf and dumb (Mark 7:32-35).

It was fascinating. Everybody plunged into the discussion. Everybody found a new angle. Quite naturally everybody found questions to ask. "Why does He sometimes touch a person and sometimes not? Why does He go into ceremonies when He proved that He can change water into wine by merely willing it, without even saying so. And . . . and . . . and . . ."

It was one of those days when the supper bell found us still sitting in the bay window. None of us had noticed the time flying, and questions were by no means all answered. Letters went back and forth whenever one of the two families found a new angle for an answer. The questions have still not all been solved. What a great consolation that St. Augustine says that what he does not know about the Gospels is so much more than what he does know!

Another time the topic was Our Lord as a story-teller. We picked out all the parables one by one:

> The story of the prodigal son
> "A sower went out to sow"
> The laborers in the vineyard
> The ten virgins
> The story of the good Samaritan
> The story of the rich man and Lazarus

And so on. In looking at them more closely, we could see great differences among them according to the audiences our Lord was addressing.

Then came the questions: "Why did He talk in parables at all? Why did He explain them at times, and at other times, not?" Quite naturally, we people of the twentieth century, the age of the short story, will admire such immortal masterpieces of story-telling as the Prodigal Son or the Good Samaritan.

Automatically this discussion led to another one, Our Lord as a teacher. There we see Him in the Sermon on the Mount instructing the multitudes, instructing communities, every so often instructing His disciples, but always following a completely new method, His very own, so that the people said in admiration: "Never did man speak like this man" (John 7:46). "For He was teaching them as one having power, and not as the scribes and Pharisees" (Matt. 7:29). It was not only the method which was so new, but most of all, it was *what* He was teaching.

For the first time people listened to the greatest news of all that there is a Father in Heaven so closely concerned about every one of them that not even a hair can fall from their heads without His knowing it.

For the first time also people listened to another piece of news. That because they are all children of the same "Father, Who art in Heaven," they must feel like sisters and brothers among each other: "Love thy neighbor as thyself."

For the first time they learned how they could themselves attain to their Father's kingdom: "The kingdom of God is like unto. . . ."

For the first time they learned about spiritual life and how to nourish it, how to regain it after it has been lost.

For the first time they learned how to become happy —not by winning friends and influencing people, but by becoming poor in spirit, pure in heart: "Blessed are they. . . ."

There is no end to the new facets one can find on the divine crystal, Jesus as a teacher.

But the same can be said about Our Lord as a leader, especially to us, the children of our times with their self-appointed Duces, Fuehrers, and Leaders.

"I couldn't imagine Christ or His mother ever having gone to a party," exclaimed a lady once. Well, if we can't imagine that, we had better look into the pages of the New Testament quickly. He went whenever He was invited, and that seems to have been quite frequently. Much too often for the taste of the Pharisees, who finally called Him disgustedly "a glutton and a wine drinker" (Matt. 11:19).

At the wedding of Cana we see Him and His mother attending one of those Oriental weddings which lasted at least a week, where there was entertainment for the guests in the form of dancing and music and speeches, much good food and even more good wine. It is very profitable to do some research work on Our Lord at parties. It makes Him so much more human.

XVII

"and certain women . . . ministered unto Him"

Some years ago I gave a lecture in a large city. During the talk it happened several times that you could have heard that famous pin drop. Afterwards there was a little party, and there I was offered the chance of a lifetime. A rich lady approached me and said:

"If you can talk like that, then you can also found a church."

She pleaded with me to found a church solely for women and be its first high priestess. Money would not matter. One million dollars would be available right away. I could also design my own vestments.

This was like a bombshell. A lively discussion followed. She complained bitterly that all the existing churches were catering to men.

"Just look at your own Church," she frowned. "The Pope, Bishops, priests—always men. Women have nothing to say during the service. That goes back to the time when Christ chose only men for His disciples. He is to be blamed for it all. He brought women to submission under men. He enslaved them as they had never been enslaved before in history. Just remember the beautiful temple services of pagan times," she exclaimed with enthusiasm, "where the high priestess conducted worship and music. We absolutely have to bring those times back!"

When I had made it unmistakably clear that she could not count on me, since I was already a member of what she had called my Church and also because I didn't believe what she said myself, she was disappointed and angry.

132

"How undignified for a woman to follow Christ!" were her last words.

When I met my family, they didn't want to believe me at first. It sounded so absurd. I had been taken completely by surprise, as much by the suggestion that I found a church as by the accusations against Christ and Christianity, and I couldn't even retaliate. I knew it was silly and wrong, but I had never done too much thinking on that point. Now we all agreed that there was a great need for some real research on Christ and women.

We had to begin by finding out about the "good old times" before Christ. Father Wasner got hold of the respective historical books from the public library, and now we studied the position of women among the old Greeks, among the Romans, among the Egyptians, the Buddhists, the Confucians. The more we read, the more we found that women were the property of men. Fathers or husbands could sell them or kill them. Men were "wisdom personified" whereas women were born stupidity, a mere zero for mankind. Nowhere in all the pagan lands and religions was there any respect for women. Classical paganism had done away completely with the dignity of womanhood. It was somewhat different among the ancient Jews. Whereas the pagans of antiquity glorified promiscuity, the Jews of the Old Testament always called a sin a sin. Marriage and family were held in high esteem. But the women themselves had just as little to say as their sisters among the pagans. The father gave his daughters in marriage without asking them. Women were restricted to running the household and caring for the little children. They were not worthy of being educated or of partaking in any of the religious ceremonies. At the time of Christ their position had become much worse. Women at that time were rather things than persons. The Rabbis couldn't insist enough on the superiority of the men. Women were inferior. They could not be legal witnesses. Women, slaves, and children were on the same level. To study the Torah—the Law of the Old Testament—was the exclusive privilege of men. A famous Rabbi coined this expression: "Rather should the Torah be burned than given in trust to a woman." The Rabbis said that one hundred women were the equivalent of two men. (That was already a great improvement on the famous Euripides, who said that ten thousand women were worth less than one man.) At the time of Christ the people of Israel had lost the ways of old when they had venerated Deborah, Judith, Esther, Ruth, Rebecca, and Rachel. Just like her pagan sisters, woman was sighing in her degradation for the coming Messiah in a two-fold way —for all her people and for women especially.

This was the state of affairs when the time was fulfilled. This was now the time of "the Woman." When everything had been spoiled for men in paradise, God Himself had pronounced this prophecy addressed to the serpent: "I will put enmities between thee and the woman" (Gen. 3: 15). The great Rabbis, teachers, and scribes did not know that when a certain little child was born in Nazareth, she had been conceived without sin and would be addressed by the angel: "Hail, full of grace." Mary is "the Woman" who will restore her sex to the dignity of the time before the fall. Her Son, venerating her in all women, will bring about this revolution which will reinstate women and place them at the side of men as it was in paradisiacal times when God said: "It is not good for man to be alone: let us make him a help *like unto himself*" (Gen. 2:18).

After He had grown up and had lived under the same roof for thirty long years with the holiest of women, He Who was the Son of God, but also the Son of Man—her Son—had the greatest respect for her whole sex. And when the time had finally come for Him to talk about the things His Father had told Him, this was among these things: that before God the soul of a woman is worth exactly as much as the soul of a man. He will teach this truth not only in words, but also by His actions.

This is one of the most revolutionary deeds in the three long years of His Public Life, that He will address women just as much as men. The Rabbis taught that a man was not even supposed to greet a woman, not even so much as look at her on the street. He had to avert his eyes. If he had bad luck and had, for instance, to ask direction of a woman, he had to do it with the fewest possible words, eyes lowered. Not only should a man not talk *with* women, but he should also not mention them at all in his speech. Now there comes Our Lord. Every so often He will choose His parables from the world of women as well as from the world of men.

For instance, after He has just likened the Kingdom of Heaven to "a grain of mustard seed which a *man* took . . ." He will liken it to "leaven which a *woman* took and hid in three measures of meal until the whole was leavened" (Matt. 13:31-33).

After He has painted the beautiful picture of the Good Shepherd Who goes tirelessly after the lost sheep, He tells immediately about the woman having ten drachmas and losing one. Does she not "light a candle and sweep the house and seek diligently until she find it?" (Luke 15:8.)

Another time the Kingdom of Heaven will be like ten virgins. . . . (Matt. 25:1-13.)

When He wants to tell them a parable—that they must pray always and not lose heart (Luke 18:1) He tells them the story of the widow and the unjust judge.

"And Jesus sitting over against the treasury, beheld how the people cast money into the treasury" (Mark 12:41). This is the second time that He places a widow as an example before His disciples. The first widow has surmounted all obstacles with her persistent heart (Luke 18:1-5). The second one will be praised for her final generosity. "She of her want cast in all she had, even her whole living" (Mark 12:44).

On that same Tuesday when Our Lord is teaching in the temple and has just told the beautiful story of the widow's mite, the Saducees also come with a "widow story": "The wife of the seven brothers." The answer they get they have most certainly not expected: that the woman just as well as her seven husbands will be equal to the angels. This is so terrific that the Gospel says: "Neither durst any man from that day forth ask him any more questions" (Matt. 22:23-33, 46).

On that same last Tuesday He tells them the story of the

father with the two sons. The father said to the first son, "Son, go work today in my vineyard," but the boy said he didn't want to. Afterwards he was sorry and went. The father went and said the same thing to the second son, who answered: "I go, Sir," but he did not go. Then He asks the question: "Which of the two did the father's will?" His unwilling audience has to say the first. And now He says the hard words: "Amen, I say to you that the publicans and the harlots shall go into the kingdom of God before you. For John came to you in the way of justice, and you did not believe him. But the publicans and harlots believed him" (Matt. 21:31-32).

Another time He threatens them that "The queen of the south shall rise in judgment with this generation and shall condemn it: because she came from the ends of the earth to hear the wisdom of Solomon. And behold a greater than Solomon here" (Matt. 12:42).

In His own home town He also starts talking about a widow, the widow Sarepta. We know that His people got so angry about it that they tried to kill Him (Luke 4:25-29).

When He warns His listeners to be watchful because "you know not the day nor the hour" (Matt. 25-13), He warns the men; "Then two shall be in the field. One shall be taken and one shall be left." Then He warns the women: "Two women shall be grinding at the mill. One shall be taken and one shall be left" (Matt. 24:40-41).

On the last day He tries to explain to them because they don't understand: "A woman, when she is in labor, hath sorrow, because her hour is come; but when she hath brought forth the child, she remembereth no more the anguish, for joy that a man is born into the world" (John 16: 21).

And then came the Sabbath on which something happened which led to a climax. St. Luke (13:11-17) tells us the story.

"And behold there was a woman who had a spirit of infirmity eighteen years. And she was bowed together: neither could she look upwards at all. Whom when Jesus saw, he called her unto Him and said to her: Woman, thou art delivered from thy infirmity. And he laid his hands upon her: and immediately she was made straight and glorified God. And the ruler of the synagogue (being angry that Jesus had healed on the sabbath) answering, said to the multitude: Six days there are wherein you ought to work. In them therefore come and be healed: and not on the sabbath day. And the Lord answering him, said: Ye hypocrites, doth not every one of you, on the sabbath day, loose his ox or his ass from the manger and lead them to water? And ought not this daughter of Abraham, whom Satan hath bound, lo, these eighteen years, be loosed from this bond on the sabbath day? And when he said these things, all his adversaries were ashamed: and all the people rejoiced for all the things that were gloriously done by him."

"DAUGHTER OF ABRAHAM!" To call Abraham one's father was the great pride of every Jew; but all over the Scriptures there was talk only of the sons of Abraham. It was Our Lord's very own invention to use the words "this daughter of Abraham." What a deep impression it made on His listeners. The ones were put to shame while the others rejoiced.

If a man was supposed not even to talk with a woman, how much less was he supposed to touch one. But there we see Jesus taking Peter's mother-in-law by the hand and curing her from the fever, and also taking the little daughter of Jairus who had died and giving her back to her parents. He Who could say to one leper: "I will, be thou clean" and he was made clean—He did not *have* to touch the women. No, He wanted to.

And how He shows His emotions for women! Out of compassion for a mother who is a widow, He raises her only son from the dead. Out of compassion for two sisters who are among His best friends, He calls forth their brother, who was four days in the tomb.

One of the most revolutionary things He ever did happened in Samaria when His disciples found Him talking to the woman at Jacob's Well. Not only that He was talking to a woman, but she was also a Samaritan. Not only was He talking to her, but He had also accepted a drink of water at her hand. And not only that, but He finally disclosed His identity to her. And the first one to whom He Himself said that He was the Messiah was this sinful stranger (John 4:4-42).

The Apostles really thought they were doing the right thing when they told the mothers harshly to go away with their little ones. After all, weren't they women? Unmistakably Our Lord taught them that they were still thinking in the ways of old, whereas He had already founded the New Covenant (Mark 10:13-17).

No Rabbi would have defiled himself in talking to a woman taken in adultery (John 8:1-11). No Rabbi would have allowed a sinful woman to touch his feet, to anoint his head (Luke 7:37-50). No Rabbi would have allowed a girl to sit in at his talks to the men, and of all things, to sit right at his feet. He also would have never allowed her sister to break in and interrupt him in the middle of his speech. Still, Mary and Martha were His closest friends (Luke 10:40-42).

The poor elderly lady who had spent all her fortune on doctors but couldn't be helped, must have heard about His great kindness to women, because she said to herself, "If I only touch His garment, I shall be healed," and she approached Him in the crowd and touched the hem of His garment (Luke 8:43-48).

His unequalled reputation traveled even across the border to the country of the Syro-Phoenicians. A mother from that country dares to approach Him, although she knows what the Jews in general think about Gentiles. Now we see Our Lord putting her off as He has once done, it seems, to His mother. This woman, also cannot be cheated, and the final outcome is that Jesus not only does what she asks of Him, but also praises her: "O woman, great is thy faith" (Matt. 15:22-28).

Therefore, we cannot be the least bit astonished when we see how women all over the country responded to the Master. A number of them even got together and, in a little club, followed Him around wherever He went, and not only that, but took care of His and the disciples' needs. "And certain women who had been healed of evil spirits and infirmities: Mary who is called Magdalen, out of whom seven devils were gone forth, and Joanna the wife of Chusa, Herod's steward, and Susanna *and many others* who ministered unto him of their substance" (Luke 8:2-3).

The sober, critical men needed a direct invitation: "Come, follow me," and after they had done so, they would still quarrel among themselves as to which one would be the greater and wonder a good deal about their reward. As Peter worded it: "Behold we have left all things and have followed thee: what therefore shall we have?" (Matt. 19:27) Women are different, although they also must have received a special vocation, because Our Lord said once: "No man can come to me, except the Father, who hath sent me, draw him" (John 6:44), and another time: "You have not chosen me: but I have chosen you" (John 15:16). That was true of the women as well as of the men in the company. All they needed, however, was the permission to stay with Him. He didn't have to give them special rewards. He knew all they wanted was to be allowed to love Him and to show their love by providing for Him. What they did was quite unusual. Their contemporaries surely couldn't have understood it. They were obviously from different walks of life. Some were noble ladies who would have left everything behind and would follow in His footsteps. This is the first real feminine movement.

Up and down throughout Galilee they follow Him, and at the end they will be under the cross. They will help to bury Him, and they will want to mourn at His grave. Little wonder it is, therefore, that after the Resurrection, Our Lord appears to the women. First, tradition tells us, to His mother, and then to Mary Magdalene (Mark 16:9).

This is a true story as it is written down in the pages of history. Against the dark background of the position of women in ancient and modern paganism, Christ stands out as a figure of light.

Mathilda Ludendorff, one of the leading names among

the Nazis, wrote a book in which she tried to prove that
Chirst is only a myth, and His teachings are ancient wisdom from India plagiarized by the Gospels. Her husband, a
famous name of his time, introduced this book with the following recommendation: "On the widespread reading of
this book depends the liberation of the individual, of the
German people, and of all peoples." The title of the book
was: *Redemption From Jesus Christ.* And her sister in
America had said it was undignified for women to follow
Christ. Mary Magdalene, however, says in the name of all
her sisters throughout the centuries: "I have seen the Lord,
and these things he said to me" (John 20:18).

XVIII

"a woman clothed with the sun . . ."

It was at the end of the summer, and our Music Camp was just over. A few of our best friends had stayed behind to help us close up. The evenings we usually spent in my little house on the campus sitting around in a circle, bay-window-fashion, talking about "it." "It" is spiritual life, which has many more aspects than there are evenings to talk them over.

One of our seminarian friends, leaned back in his chair and said rather helplessly:

"I don't know what I can do. I have absolutely no feeling for the Blessed Mother. Try as I may—I have read many books about her but she seems to me a perfect stranger. She is so completely unreal. That makes me so sad, but what can one do?"

We had spent so much time with the Holy Family in Nazareth, seeing the mother of the house as a real house wife, cooking, washing, baking bread, cleaning house, preparing and mending garments, and all the while mothering a little Boy. Now we told Stanislaus all about it. How very, very real she was!

Then we came to talk about one of the most beautiful stories in all the Gospels, the one of the marriage feast in Cana in Galilee, when Mary, the mother of Jesus, was there. The Gospel continues, "And Jesus also was invited" (John 2:2). At that time He had not made a name for Himself yet. He and His disciples were obviously invited on account of His mother, to whose family the newly-weds

must have belonged. Mary is usually described in word
and picture as a rather shy, retiring person, clad in complete silence. The faraway look in her eyes indicates that
she was pondering in her heart, which seems to make her
oblivious of what is going on around her. All these artists
of pen and brush seem to feel it a sacrilege to let her stoop
down so low as to little trifles of everyday life. As the
words of Holy Scriptures are inspired by the Holy Ghost, we
can confidently take the story of the wedding of Cana as
a most valuable aid to a true biography of Mary.

"And the wine failing, the mother of Jesus saith to
him . . ." (John 2:3). To appreciate what that means,
we have to understand all the customs of such a marriage
feast of her time, how the friend of the bridegroom was the
steward who was also in charge of the wine, and who was
most solicitous that everything should go as well as possible. It had escaped his attention, but it had not escaped
her motherly vigilance. What really happened is this.
Through the thoughtlessness of somebody, the wine was
alarmingly short, which would amount to a great embar-
rassment for the hosts. Mary does not think this is a trifle
too little to bother her Son with. As a real housewife, as a
real mother, she foresees this painful situation. Had she
been like most of her statues with eyes and hands raised to
heaven, she wouldn't even have noticed what was going on.

No, she must have been up and around, coming and going, watching and seeing everything, and before anybody
else, she anticipated the need and "did something about
it." How heartwarming! And again, how real and how close
she becomes. When her Son in His answer which does not
sound encouraging to us, but didn't disturb her a bit, calls
her "Woman," many people like Stanislaus wonder and
don't understand. So we mentioned that last day in Eden
to Stanislaus, when God Almighty Himself gives her this
greatest of all titles in His prophecy about "the Woman"
(Gen. 3:15). And what authority she had! As was usually the case, the women belonging to the wedding party
assembled at the house days ahead of time baking and
preparing. Maybe Mary had taken over the leadership

among them. With what natural poise she now steps over to
the servants and commands: "Whatsoever he shall say to
you, do ye." Perhaps the servants may have laughed outright at the funny idea of filling those huge stone jars with
water at the end of a feast when there would be no more
ablutions; but because of her words, they went back and
forth many times with their pitchers, filling the jars.
Doesn't she still do the same thing today? Looking imploringly at us, she says: "Do whatever He tells you." How can
we refuse her pleading and not listen to Him when He
says, "Love ye one another as I have loved you."

Stanislaus had already said repeatedly that this was all
new to him, and it had never occurred to him just like that.
He seemed to grow happier and the tense, anxious expression on his face vanished visibly.

While we were telling and explaining, I got one of those
fits against this degenerate sacred art of Barclay Street.
How should a young man of our days get any access to a
person represented in these doll-like faces, clad in pastel
colors, whose lily-white hands seem only meant to be folded
but couldn't be imagined as kindling a fire or washing a
little Boy's clothes or taking care of a carpenter's household. It seems to me that heresies don't absolutely have to
be preached or printed; they can also be painted or carved
in stone. These cute and sweetish representations of Mary
are a heresy widely spread.

And then we came to the end of the Gospels. We see
Mary as a warm-blooded woman, mothering not only her
own Child but anyone who was in need—when it comes
to the Passion of Our Lord, the Holy Ghost lets us have
a look into the depths of her heart. "Did you not
know?" her Son had said to her once when she hadn't
quite understood Him. That had been twenty-one years
ago. In these years she had been pondering in her
heart on everything He had said and done. She also
had advanced in grace to such heights that He never would
have to say to her any more: "Did you not know?" (Luke
2:49.) She always understood. We see her now in the most
cruel suffering a mother can endure: her Son caught like

a criminal, betrayed by one of His own, denied by one of His best friends, mocked, ridiculed, and treated with the utmost scorn, scourged, tortured, disfigured, and finally condemned to death. Mary knew what power as a mother she might have over human hearts, how irresistible she would be if she were to step up to Pilate who was wavering anyhow, how she could perhaps turn the fury of the multitudes into pity.

She understood. And while her heart was pierced by the sword, she kept silently in the background. Simon was allowed to help carry the cross; Veronica might comfort Him with her veil; the holy women could show their grief so that He even stopped and addressed them—the mother could only exchange a silent look. Then when the Gospel says: "Now there stood by the cross of Jesus, his mother. . . . he saith to his mother: Woman, behold thy son" (John 19:25-26), it was the final approval of Jesus towards His mother. The prophecy was fulfilled. Here she stands: the Woman.

XIX

today

In the beginning of the book I told you how it happened that we became interested in the life of Christ, in reconstructing it for ourselves as closely as possible day by day as it may have happened nineteen hundred years ago. Then in the next chapters I tried to tell how we did what we did by showing you some of our versions of the Childhood Story and the Hidden Life. Then I picked at random some of the countless aspects of Our Lord's personality through which He was observed when we read the Gospels together throughout the years, alone and with our friends.

And now I want to tell you about still another discovery which we made when we had already become quite familiar with Our Lord. This happened when one blessed day we seemed to understand what St. Paul meant when he exclaimed: "Jesus Christ, yesterday and today, and the same forever" (Heb. 13:8); and in another place: "I live, now not I; but Christ liveth in me" (Gal. 2:20). These two statements were linked up with that tremendous statement the mysterious voice had made to Paul when he was still Saul: "I am Jesus whom thou persecutest" (Acts 9:5). From that day on these words became the whole pattern for our life.

If He can be identified with each one of us and *if* He is the same yesterday as today—then He just continues His very life in every one of us until the end of time. Maybe this is why the Church introduces the reading of the Gospel at Holy Mass with: *"Initium sancti Evangelii,"* and *"Sequentia sancti Evangelii,"* but never *"Finis sancti Evan-*

145

gelii''; the Gospels are not finished yet, and we are a part of them.

It is a big moment when one realizes that. One feels like saying: "All right, dear Lord, here are my hands and feet, eyes and ears, my lips and my heart—they are Yours." I suppose this is the first step towards the final goal: "I live, now not I, but Christ liveth in me."

As soon as one becomes familiar with the fact that He is the same today as yesterday, one will meet Him constantly with His friends and stories, He really is the same. Nothing has changed. The Good Shepherd is still going after the lost sheep; the Father is still waiting for the Prodigal Son; Mary Magdalen is still sitting at His feet after He has freed her from seven devils.

It may be that not everybody will come across Mary Magdalen or the Good Shepherd in a drastic way. But as soon as we have awakened to what the words mean: "Jesus Christ, yesterday, and today"; and as soon as we want to meet Him *today,* we can always—always find Him unerringly as Jesus, "the Man of Sorrows and acquainted with infirmity" (Isa. 53:3). Once He would talk about the persecuted Christians of the first decade: "I am Jesus whom thou persecutest" (Acts 9:5). This is true throughout the centuries. All we have to do is to learn to think about our fellow men in that term: "I am Jesus."

There are those incredible stories which seep through the Iron Curtain, which tell us how He re-lives His whole Passion, how He is again scourged and crowned with thorns, "Depised and the most abject of men" (Isa. 53:3), crucified and pierced by the lance. And this is not one story; there must be thousands like it now.

If they seem a little remote to us, let us look around and we might find Him in the same unbloody persecutions as He had to endure by the Pharisees: in our high schools and colleges, in offices, in newspapers and magazines. If we just learn to look, we shall find Him, and again He says, "I am Jesus whom thou persecutest." As we look into the lives of our friends and neighbors, how much suffering do we find! And the great day will come when we discover the cross in our own life. Up to then we may have hated it, but on that glorious day we shall understand His words: "If any man will come after me, let him deny himself and take up his cross daily and follow me" (Luke 9:23). On that blessed day we shall suddenly know that it is He Himself Who wants to suffer in us, Who wants to give us that greatest of all privileges: to help to "fill up those things that are wanting of the sufferings of Christ" (Col. 1:24). This is a mystery as great as the Incarnation or the Blessed Trinity. We shall never quite understand how it can be that we are called upon to co-operate in the work of the Redemption, but so it is. We can only faintly understand it when we think of the *Corpus Christi Mysticum,* the Mystical Body of Christ, of which He is the head and we are the members. And this whole *Corpus Christi* is suffering throughout the ages until the measure of suffering is fulfilled.

What we once said of Mary and Joseph, how they are still going from house to house seeking shelter, we can now say of the Son of Man. He is still carrying His cross, and we meet Him every day. Do we want to hold it with the scribes and elders, saying: "If he be the king of Israel, let him now come down from the cross: and we will believe him" (Matt. 27:42), or translated into our language, "If there were a God, there couldn't be this awful war. How can God allow so much unhappiness?"

Or do we want to be Veronica? Because again He identifies Himself this time with the least of His brethren, and whatever we do to this one, He will count as having been done unto Him (Matt. 25:40).

Encountering Him TODAY we may come across fantastic situations but, after all, hasn't His whole life been full of such fantastic events, and haven't we discovered that His life is going on in our very days? So don't be astonished when, after you have studied the life of Christ in Palestine, you discover it again in Vermont, Chicago, New York and other places.

XX

a letter

Stowe, Vermont
April, 1951

Dear Friends:

It was the end of January, 1951. Our Christmas vacation was over, and the great blue bus came from New York to get us for our concert tour to the west coast. There was the usual hustle and bustle of stowing all the many things into the bus, this time even a baby crib for Werner's little Barbara. There was the running back and forth with all the last-minute errands. There was Dave blowing the horn and shouting "All aboard!", and when the bus finally rolled out of the courtyard, there was Martina standing on the porch next to her husband Jean, waving, half happy, half sad. This was the first time she would not be with us in all those many years of singing. That was sad. But when we should come back from the west coast at the end of April, there would be a little baby lying in the cradle upstairs. Martina had brought this old, wood-carved cradle along from Salzburg this past summer, and now she was fixing it for her first child. So this was a farewell with a tear and a smile.

Four weeks later we drove into one of those large, modern motor courts in Wasco, California. It was a Sunday night, the end of February. We had had an afternoon concert, after which we had driven on to the next concert town, and now we would have a quiet Sunday evening together. This and the fact that we all prefer these beautiful motor courts to any hotel, put us in the best of spirits. The man at the desk in the office said that a long-distance call was waiting for us. When he said, "You should call Operator 14 in Morrisville, Vermont," we knew the call came from home. It must be something very urgent.

We placed a call, and very shortly afterward, the operator said: "Here is your party; go ahead."

And a voice at the other end sobbed into the telephone: "Mother—Martina is dead."

This is one of those moments where the heart actually seems to stop, and everything around one disappears in darkness.

The connection was not good, and all we could understand was that the baby had started to come four weeks too early, but the doctor was glad, because it was large. Martina was in the hospital. Everything went fine at the beginning until complications arose which made it necessary for the docotr to suggest an operation. The baby died right away after it was baptized. Martina seemed all right. The operation was over, the doctors were gone. Martina was just beginning to wake up from the anaesthesia, when all of a sudden, her heart stopped. And could we come home now, please.

Meanwhile, the family had gotten settled in their different cottages, getting ready for a quiet Sunday evening. Now I had to tell them. I sent little Johannes around with the message that everybody should come immediately to Cabin #6.

We knelt down and said the first Rosary for our dear little Martina, all of us numb and still without understanding what that meant: Martina is dead.

Now we had to attend to practical matters: airplane tickets to Burlington. Dave, who was deeply shocked, went to the telephone and returned soon with the unexpected news: "Every space is taken. They can put you on the waiting list. The earliest chance will be in three days." That meant we had to give up the idea of all of us going home.

But I implored Dave: "Please try to get at least one seat for me." After hours of anxious waiting, one seat was secured, leaving Los Angeles at eight o'clock the next morning. But we were far from Los Angeles. I had to drive fifty miles to the next airport, from where a plane would take me at two o'clock in the morning down south. When I was getting ready to leave, the family gathered around me handing me letters "for Martina," as tears streamed down their faces. Father Wasner and Dave went along to the airport. Then—a last good-bye, a last blessing, and I was alone. There was a long night and a long day until the plane got into LaGuardia Field. One of our close priest friends was waiting for me.

"The connecting plane to Burlington has left already, and you have to stay overnight in New York. But tomorrow we shall come with you." I was deeply touched and very grateful in Martina's name when I learned that six priests would attend her funeral.

The closer the moment came when I should meet Jean and Pierre and Therese and Martina, the more I dreaded it. But when I finally stood at her side, looking down on her beautiful face, I felt a strange peace coming over me, which seemed to emanate from Martina. There she was lying where her father had lain before in our big living room in her wedding dress with an imperceptible, tiny smile around her lips. At her feet in a small white coffin slept little Notburga, her child.

And then we sat together, Jean and I, holding each other's hands. There was not very much to tell. The doctors didn't know themselves. Martina, who had never been sick in all her life, had been well to the very last moment. The doctors didn't even think that it was an embolism. They just frankly didn't know. A Caesarian operation is usually nothing to worry about nowadays. It is being done successfully all the time.

"God wanted her," Jean said quietly. After a long silence he added, "She was too good to live very much longer. I had had that feeling often lately. She is in Heaven. Poor Jean. He had been so happy, and now, in an instant, he had lost wife and child.

Then we had to attend to practical matters. Jean said, "Mother, let's do everything ourselves. I know Martina would want it that way.'' His two brothers, Pierre and Jacques, went out to the graveyard to dig the grave. First they had to clear away six feet of snow, which was lucky in a way, because the soil under so much snow was not frozen very deep. The end of February is still deepest winter, and very cold up here in Vermont.

Jean and Martina had been helping Wayne, the carpenter, during the last weeks, finishing the new wing, and Wayne, like everybody else, had grown very fond of Martina and was, like everybody else, also deeply shocked. Jean asked Wayne now to make a coffin for Martina in old-world style out of white pine boards with a big cross on the lid, the cross stained dark. The funeral was set for Thursday at ten o'clock. I sent a telegram to the west coast, where I knew that ten anxious hearts were waiting for news: "OUR DEAR MARTINA AND HER LITTLE NOTBURGA WILL BE BURIED THURSDAY TEN O'CLOCK." I knew they would sing a Requiem at the same time in California as we would in Stowe.

Telegrams and letters came, and flowers started pouring in, and friends arrived. There was always someone with Martina. Prayers were said in French, in German, in English. In spite of the bad road on our hill and of the bitter cold, people came from all around. The telephone rang constantly with people from the village offering their cars, their help. It was a great comfort in such bottomlessly sad hours to feel such compassion. In the evenings the living room was filled. During the day we gathered a couple of times in the bay window, looking over at Martina, rehearsing the Requiem High Mass. From a near-by college the choir had offered to sing it but—"Let's do everything ourselves," we had said. "Martina would like it better that way." With the singing family way out in California, I was a little bit worried as to how it would go, but when Father McDonnell arrived, who is choir director in his seminary, all was well, and I am sure Martina would like it.

On Wednesday Rupert came with Rosmarie, who had stayed with him, helping him around the house and with the children. Now there was at least one brother and one sister with Martina. With Rupert also came Anne Marie, one of his sisters-in-law.

In the evenings Father McDonough, our pastor, came over, leading the Rosary and giving a little talk on the liturgy of a Christian burial, which is so very consoling, and how the first Christians had looked at death. Instead of mourning, they celebrated a feast, the birthday of their beloved one in Heaven. Instead of expressing their sympathy, they congratulated the bereaved. Some of this spirit we could feel descending upon us more and more.

On Wednesday the coffin arrived. We put it on the table in the music room and lined it with fresh balsam twigs and flowers. In the evening after the last prayer was said, we all went in and, standing around the coffin, we said one Our Father for the next one in our midst to die. This is an old Tyrolean custom, and it is a real *memento mori*. It makes one realize in a very straight-to-the-point way that one day it will be for us, and one just hopes that there will also be a group of friends around helping with their prayers.

Friends kept coming until past midnight. This is the mercy of these days. There are so many arrangements to be made, so many things to be thought about, and that, too, is a great help. Pierre and Therese, who had been married with Martina and Jean on the same day, really outdid themselves in arranging everything "as Martina would like it."

Jean dreaded the black hearse and was sure Martina would not like to be put in there, so Rupert and the others decorated our Jeep truck with carpets and evergreens. After a last prayer at Martina's side, all the friends went to get their coats, while we placed Martina on her last bed of flowers and fragrant balsam, placing little Notburga in the arm of her mother, covering them both with the rich folds of her bridal veil. Then we went down the hill to the little wooden church, at the threshold of which Father McDonough awaited Martina. As we entered the church, we sang: *"Subvenite sancti Dei, occurrite angeli Domini. . . ."* (Come, ye saints of God, meet us, oh angels of the

Lord, take her soul and offer her to the presence of the Highest.) And now with the words and music of the Requiem we understood again what is meant by the words "Holy Mother Church." No one can console like a mother, and no one can console and help better than this great Mother of us all, the Church. "Eternal rest grant to her, Oh Lord," she says, "and may perpetual light shine upon her."

When we left the church, it was snowing in big white flakes, and when we came to the cemetery, the little mound of fresh dirt next to the grave was covered with a white blanket.

At the same time, the rest of the family went into the Catholic church in Coalinga, California, thinking they would quietly, all by themselves, sing a Requiem; but when they arrived, the church was filled. Word had gotten around. All the school children had come, and many other people. And so it turned out to be a manifold *"Requiem eternam dona eis Domine"* which went up to the throne of God. At such moments one feels suddenly that this is what we meant when we say in the Creed, we believe in the Communion of Saints; when all these perfect strangers turn into sisters and brothers, co-members of the Church Militant, uniting in prayer.

After we had all filed past the open grave with our last gift of blessed earth and holy water, we went back to the house. Everybody was half frozen. A roaring fire was kindled in the fireplace, and hot lunch was served.

In the morning mail was a letter from a very dear friend, Reverend Father Abbot of the Trappists. It said: "We envy you your sorrow and Martina her Heaven."

As the snowstorm increased, many of the guests wanted to leave before it should be too difficult to get down the hill. I had to fly back the same night to San Francisco. Before leaving for the airport, I wanted to sit once more with Jean. He had been really wonderful all these days, so truly resigned to the Will of God. Now he told me how Martina had used all the money I had sent her for her birthday two weeks before for Austrian Relief packages.

Jean said he would send all the baby things Martina had
so lovingly prepared for little Notburga to Austria to be
given to a very poor mother with the request to call the
child Martin or Martina. That had been very hard to see
—the nursery all prepared, the room next to their bed-
room, with all those sweet little things lying around, waiting. I had been worried whether it wouldn't be too much
for Jean to look at it from now on, so I asked him with a
heavy heart what he planned to do next. He said he
would go home to Montreal with his mother for a few
days, and then he wanted to work hard and long hours,
and so he intended to help that famous garden architect
who had made that beautiful rock garden in front of our
house. Working with rocks for the whole day, he thought
he might be able to sleep. I felt greatly relieved. I knew
how terribly quiet our big house can be when everybody is
gone. That matters very little as long as there are two of
you, but when the beloved is gone, never to return, then
one discovers what "alone" means. For this there is no real
remedy, but prayer and work help us to carry this cross.

And then I was on my way back to California in the
airplane, alone with my thoughts. When Martina had been
a little girl, she had said time and again, "I don't want to
be a grownup ever. I always want to be little." God had
really granted her that wish—outwardly and inwardly.
That showed most in her uncomplicated, childlike piety.
"We should be so continuously grateful for what God has
done for us that the least we can give Him in return is
all," she wrote once to Jean.

During the last years when I was quite sick, she had always taken care of me, spent weeks with me in the hospital and nursed me back to health, always patient, always
cheerful, full of little surprises. A little bouquet of wild
flowers, still wet with dew, picked at sunrise, or a hand-
painted little card, in which art she was a master. Once in
those days she had confided to me that she was afraid to
die. Now I had to think that God in His love and mercy
had spared His child this last fright. He called her at the
moment of her greatest happiness, when she expected to
wake up and find her child in her arms. Now I tried to

picture Martina's real awakening, being greeted by her holy child, her mother and father and little sisters and brothers. In my prayer book is a holy card with the words of St. Jerome from a letter of consolation addressed to his friend, St. Paula, representing her dead daughter Blesilla as saying, "Dear Mother, if you desire my welfare, trouble not my peace and joy by your tears. You fancy perhaps that I am lonely, but I live in such good company. I am with Mary the Mother of Our Lord and the holy women mentioned in the Gospel. You pity me for leaving the world, but now it is I rather who feel sorry for you and all our family because you still linger in the prison of the flesh and daily have to contend with the host of enemies who are seeking to destroy you."

And on another one are the words of St. John Chrysostom: "You complain that you suffer, having lost her who was the joy of your life. Listen, my good friend. Suppose you had given your daughter in marriage to some good and honorable man who went with her to a distant country and made her rich and happy. Would not her happiness soothe the grief you feel at the separation? How can you dare to weep and refuse to be comforted, since your child has been taken to Himself by God our Lord and King, and not by any earthly friend or relative?"

It was Friday late in the afternoon when I arrived in San Francisco. When we approached the airport and I could discover the people waiting for the airplane down there, I looked for red stockings in the crowd, but there were none. Then I looked for a Roman collar or a driver's cap, thinking that Father Wasner or Dave might have come, but there was no collar and no cap to be seen. How would I get the fifty miles to Los Gatos, where we had the concert that night? What a happy surprise it was then when an officer approached me with outstretched arms and a warm smile, and I recognized Father Saunders, the Army Chaplain who had for years helped us most generously in our Austrian Relief work when he was stationed in Salzburg. While he was driving me to Los Gatos, I told him all about Martina, and then we talked about Heaven.

I had just an hour to tell the family all about the last

days, and then it was time for the concert. Afterwards
Father Saunders joined us in saying one more Rosary
for Martina, and then at midnight, with the beginning of
Saturday, we sang "Holy God, We Praise Thy Name,"
congratulating Martina on her true birthday.

The weeks passed, and when the concert tour was over,
we returned home. There is an empty place at the family
table now, and an empty room, and there is a fresh grave
in the cemetery, which we visit every day, and where a red
vigil light is burning in a lantern during the night. The
wound is wide open again.

When the cross gets very heavy, it is good to remember
what St. Aloysius Gonzaga wrote to his mother eleven days
before his death: "I beg you, my honored Mother, be care-
ful and don't withstand God's infinite goodness by bewailing as dead one who will live in God's presence and be able
to benefit you by his prayer far more than was possible
here. Our separation will not last long. We shall see one another again in Heaven and rejoice incessantly, being united
with our Redeemer."

And now, my dear friends, we want to thank you also
in Martina's name for all your prayers and words of comfort. Let us continue to pray for one another, especially
for the one who will be next in our midst.

Yours gratefully,
THE TRAPP FAMILY

It was about six weeks after Martina's death. We were at
home all by ourselves. It was in the evening at what we call
our "social hour." We made up our family mind to spend
the time between supper and evening prayer every night
together around the fireplace, instead of vanishing into our
different private quarters. We should really not be in
Stowe, but on the ship on the way to Australia. But the only
one leaving from Vancouver was canceled, and for the
second time, our tour to Australia and New Zealand has
been postponed. This unforeseen vacation we enjoy
wholeheartedly. During the day we help finish the new

wing, carpeting and painting, and in the evenings we spend a most comfortable hour together. Some are knitting or mending stockings, Werner is weaving belts on an ingenious handmade loom, which got him the nickname "Navajo Chief." Johannes is either whittling or playing with Flockie, his Airdale terrier. Father Wasner is copying music, which doesn't hinder him from listening to what is being talked about or read aloud, because he can do more than one thing at a time. I am either reading aloud from the day's mail, or knitting on Maria's sweater, a rather belated Christmas present.

On one of those evenings it was that Johannes suddenly asked: "Can Martina see us now?"

That started it.

"Yes," I said, "I'm sure she can. Aren't you?" And I looked questioningly from one to the other.

"Sure I am," said Lorli, "But what I want to know is, how that works. If the body is buried, how can the soul see and hear?"

"Does Martina remember everything from her life here on earth, or—does she care to remember now?" asked Hedwig.

"And if she is in Heaven now, exactly what might she be doing all the time?" inquired Johannes. "Can she play with her little baby, or does she have to stand before the throne of God all the time?"

"What do children do in Heaven, the same as the grown-ups?"

"How would she recognize Father in Heaven without a body?"

All of a sudden each single one of us discovered a great many burning questions within himself, but just at this moment the bell rang for evening prayer in our chapel. Someone suggested looking into Holy Scriptures for whatever answers we could find. So we divided the different books of the New Testament among us, leaving the whole Old Testament to Father Wasner. Each one was to search his portion for whatever references he could find to life after death.

All of us say most earnestly every day when we recite the Apostles' Creed that "we believe in the resurrection of the body and life everlasting, amen." But now we had seen how many "what," "where," "when," and "how's" there are still left to ask. Together we now looked for the answers, and this is what happened.

THREE

FOREVER

XXI

blessed are the dead

When we met again and each one brought what he had found on Life Everlasting in the pages of Holy Scriptures, we were perfectly amazed at the amount to be found. If we only listed quotations, it would make many, many typewritten pages. Once the interest is aroused in what the Catechism calls "the last things," Death, Judgment, Heaven, and Hell, one cannot stop pondering about it any more. We looked through our library. We found some highly interesting books: *In Heaven We Know Our Own*, by Blot (Benziger); *What Becomes of the Dead* by Arendzen (Sheed & Ward); and a little old-fashioned-looking book in German by Dr. Robert Klimsch: *Leben die Toten* ("Do the Dead Live"—a collection of sworn testimonies in Beatification Processes).

When we talked these things over—not only in one evening but during weeks and months and ever since then, now and again—there were always two effects noticeable in the soul: first, a great consolation; and second, a greater awareness of the fact that what we are pondering about now, we are going to meet one day. There is nothing really certain in our life—except death. This is the only—really the only thing I can be sure of. I will die some day. And how will that be?

I am most grateful now for a personal experience of my own of some years ago: I *almost* died. I had been very sick, and now the end—as the doctor thought—had come. One understands that time is running short, and only in time can we do anything for Him, so every moment is precious to express one's love and one's complete resignation to the Will of the Father.

People don't realize how cruel they are in their wrongly-understood "consideration" when they keep the priest away as long as possible from their beloved sick in order "not to excite them." They don't know that they deprive their beloved ones of the greatest consolation. "Is any man sick among you?" writes St. James the Apostle. "Let him bring in the elders of the church, and let them pray over him, anointing him with oil in the name of the Lord. And the prayer of faith shall save the sick man, and the Lord shall raise him up, and if he be in sins, they shall be forgiven him" (James, 5:14-15).

I was alone in the hospital in Vienna, my family hundreds of miles away sailing in the Adria. As I lay there with eyes closed, waiting for death, I heard the doctor say to the nurse that it wouldn't make any sense to try to contact the family. It was definitely too late for them to reach me. Although the doctor talked in a whisper, I could hear him very clearly. All my senses seemed to merge and concentrate into the one sense of hearing. I noticed that while I was opening my eyes wide, I could see nothing, although it was ten o'clock in the morning. Sight was gone. I heard the rustle of the sheets as the nurse removed them from the foot of my bed, and I heard her hand gliding over my feet and her voice when she said, "Her feet area already cold," but I couldn't feel it. Touch was gone.

I heard the doctor say he would give me a camphor injection, and I heard the click of the needle; and although camphor has such a strong odor, I didn't smell it. That was gone.

"Am I dying?" I wanted to ask, but I couldn't move, couldn't speak. And then hearing also stopped, and there was a silence more intense than any silence I can remember. The body might be helpless, but the soul was wide awake and in full possession of its faculties. Undisturbed by the outside, memory was keener than ever before. And in this anguish of a last agony the soul passed once more through it past life, seeing everything so much more clearly. Although nothing is to be seen, the soul senses very sharply the presence of an evil power which wants to influence it to give up: the sins are too many and too horrible to allow of any hope. But it also senses another spiritual power present. It may be the Guardian Angel, soothing the soul, reminding it: "If your sins be as scarlet, they shall be made as white as snow: if they be red as crimson, they shall be white as wool" (Isa. 1:18); reminding the soul of the bottomless mercy and love of the Heavenly Father Whom it is to meet very soon now.

And then? Well, I did not die. But for the rest of my life I shall be grateful for those most precious moments. The nurse told me afterwards that for a little while they thought I was already dead.

Afterwards I found out that this seems to be a general occurrence and not just my private experience. They say the senses die slowly, one by one. Therefore, we should take great care what is said and done in the presence of the dying. While they are fighting their last decisive battle, it would mean such a help if they could hear us talk to them about the mercy of God, about having trust and confidence. One day we shall have to take that same step, too. This might be the best preparation. And when everything is over and one of our beloved has died, we should remember the words of the Revelation of St. John: "In those days I heard a voice from Heaven saying to me: Write: Blessed are the dead, who die in the Lord. From henceforth, now, saith the Spirit, that they may rest from their labors, for their works follow them" (Rev. 14:13).

XXII

the judgment

"It is appointed unto men once to die, and after this the judgment," writes St. Paul to the Hebrews (9:27).

The Judgment! What do we know about it? We know that we shall face two different judgments, one immediately after death, the Particular Judgment, and one at the end of time, together with all mankind, the General Judgment. "Blessed are the clean of heart: for they shall see God" (Matt. 5-8). At the very moment after our death we see ourselves *exactly* as we are. If during the last moments while we were still breathing, our life has passed by in review, then after death our whole life is seen at once as in a flash, and it is seen *sub specie aeternitatis*—"as it will be seen for all eternity." Happenings and things which may have been of great value to us while we were alive may dwindle into nothingness, and what we had thought of as little trifles may take on giant significance. At this very moment we shall perceive the justice of our future: the damned will be completely convinced that Hell is the only place for them; saints will want to fly to God like a particle of iron to a strong magnet; and the ones who are not utterly cleansed yet, whose souls still carry stains of sin, will know that nothing unclean can enter the Kingdom of God, that "no fornicator, or unclean, or covetous person . . . hath inheritance in the kingdom of Christ and of God" (Eph. 5:5). They could not stand the presence of God, Who is purity itself. Willingly will they descend into Purgatory, where they can wait in suffering till they "repay the last farthing" (Matt. 5:26).

At this decisive moment we shall not only be judged, we

shall also meet our Judge. The ones as perfect as the Heavenly Father is perfect, will meet Him right away face to face. The damned will also recognize Him, and at the same instant they will want to flee from Him in terror. Who will "the One" be: the Triune God, or Christ? Let us look at what St. Paul has to say:

"We will not have you ignorant, brethren, concerning them that are asleep, that you be not sorrowful, even as others who have no hope; for if we believe that Jesus died and rose again, even so them who have slept through Jesus, will God bring with him. For this we say unto you in the word of the Lord, that we who are alive, who remain unto the coming of the Lord, shall not prevent them who have slept. For the Lord himself shall come down from heaven with commandment, and with the voice of an archangel, and with the trumpet of God; and the dead who are in Christ shall rise first. Then we who are alive, who are left, shall be taken up together with them in the clouds to meet Christ, into the air, and so shall we be always with the Lord. Wherefore comfort ye one another with these words" (I Thess. 4:12-17).

The Scriptures say that the Father has given all judgment to the Son. Will it be Christ and the soul alone? Will the Guardian Angel be there? *"Lex orandi, lex credendi"* (As we pray, so do we believe), it is said. And in the Requiem Mass it says at the Offertory: "May Thy holy standard bearer, Michael, lead them unto the holy light." During the burial the Church prays, "Come to his assistance, ye saints of God, meet him, ye angels of the Lord, receiving his soul." And, "At the departure of thy soul from the body, may the glorious choir of angels meet thee," prays the priest over the dying. We get a glimpse of what tremendous supernatural solemnities are taking place around a deathbed. The room where a Christian has died is truly a sanctuary.

About the Last Judgment we are quite well informed by Our Lord Jesus Christ Himself.

"And when the Son of man shall come in his majesty,

and all the angels with him, then shall he sit upon the seat of his majesty.

"And all nations shall be gathered together before him: and he shall separate them one from another, as the shepherd separateth the sheep from the goats:

"And he shall set the sheep on his right hand, but the goats on his left.

"Then shall the king say to them that shall be on his right hand: Come, ye blessed of my Father, possess you the kingdom prepared for you from the foundation of the world.

"For I was hungry, and you gave me to eat: I was thirsty, and you gave me to drink: I was a stranger, and you took me in:

"Naked, and you covered me: sick, and you visited me: I was in prison, and you came to me.

"Then shall the just answer him, saying: Lord, when did we see thee hungry and feed thee: thirsty and gave thee drink?

"And when did we see thee a stranger and took thee in? Or naked and covered thee?

"Or when did we see thee sick or in prison and came to thee?

"And the king answering shall say to them: Amen I say to you, as long as you did it to one of these my least brethren, you did it to me.

"Then he shall say to them also that shall be on his left hand: Depart from me, you cursed, into everlasting fire, which was prepared for the devil and his angels.

"For I was hungry and you gave me not to eat: I was thirsty and you gave me not to drink.

"I was a stranger and you took me not in: naked and you covered me not: sick and in prison and you did not visit me.

"Then they also shall answer him, saying: Lord, when did we see thee hungry or thirsty or a stranger or naked or sick or in prison and did not minister to thee?

"Then he shall answer them, saying: Amen, I say to you, as long as you did it not to one of these least, neither did you do it to me.

"And these shall go into everlasting punishment: but the just, into life everlasting" (Matt. 25:31-46).

"Why must we be judged again if we are judged immediately after our death?" asked Johannes.

The answer is that on the last day we shall rise from the dead and the Last Judgment will be after the Resurrection of the Body. Body and soul will be reunited, and we shall be judged as full men. After the Ascension of Our Lord, the angel said to the Apostles, "This Jesus who is taken up from you into heaven, shall so come as you have seen him going into heaven" (Acts 1:11). "And they shall see the Son of man coming in the clouds of heaven with much power and majesty" (Matt. 24:30) to "judge the living and the dead" (Credo).

All of mankind, from Adam and Eve to the very last one, shall be assembled, and the hearts of men shall lie bare for all to see. Tradition says that the Last Judgment will be on earth on the very scene of Our Lord's greatest humiliation, between the Garden of Olives and Calvary. From the Scriptures we know that all the angels, the good ones and the evil ones, will be present. "The angels who kept not their principality, but forsook their own habitation, he hath reserved under darkness in everlasting chains unto the judgment of the great day" (Jude 6). All of God's intelligent creation will be there. Christ will sit on His throne, and His Apostles will also sit on twelve thrones to judge.

"And I saw a great white throne, and one sitting upon it, from whose face the earth and heaven fled away, and there was no place found for them.

"And I saw the dead, great and small, standing in the presence of the throne, and the books were opened; and another book was opened, which is the book of life: and the dead were judged by those things which were written in the books, according to their works.

"And the sea gave up the dead that were in it: and death and hell gave up their dead that were in them. And they were judged, every one according to their works.

"And hell and death were cast into the pool of fire. This is the second death.

"And whosoever was not found written in the book of life was cast into the pool of fire.

"And I saw a new heaven and a new earth. For the first heaven and the first earth was gone: and the sea is now no more.

"And I, John, saw the holy city, the new Jerusalem, coming down out of heaven from God, prepared as a bride adorned for her husband.

"And I heard a great voice from the throne, saying; Behold the tabernacle of God with men: and he will dwell with them. And they shall be his people: and God himself with them shall be their God.

"And God shall wipe away all tears from their eyes: and death shall be no more. Nor mourning, nor crying, nor sorrow shall be any more: for the former things are passed away" (Rev. 20:11-15;21:1-4).

XXIII

"Begone, Satan!"

The best preparation for a discussion of Hell is a meditation on Heaven. Hell is the complete absence, and also forever and ever, of everything Heaven is. Our Lord Who
said of Himself: "I am meek and humble of heart"
(Matt. 11:29), Who said "Come to me, all ye who labor
and are burdened and I will refresh you" (Matt. 11:28)
after Whom the multitudes were flocking because of His
endless mercy and kindness—He mentions Hell thirty-
seven times in the Gospels. St. John the Evangelist says
at the end of his Gospel that if he were to tell all he
remembers, the world would not contain all the books.
That gives us the right to take what *is* written down as
only a kind of "table of contents," and multiply it to our
hearts' content. Therefore, He may have talked very much
more often about this most serious subject: the place
"where their worm dieth not and the fire is not extin-
guished" and where "there shall be weeping and gnashing
of teeth" (Mark 9:45; Matt. 8:12; Luke 13:28).

Hell is a mystery. It is the answer to the *mysterium iniquitatis* whereby man with an act of his free will in cool
consideration chooses to do without God. To this the only
logical consequence is Hell. Time and again one hears people object to the fact of eternal Hell as being unworthy of
a kind Heavenly Father Who could not possibly torture
His children thus forever. This is merely sentimental, and
only shows that these people have not yet comprehended
what it means that we are created with a free will. In complete freedom we choose Hell. We are not pushed into it.

What has been said of Heaven, that it has not "entered

169

into the heart of man, what things God hath prepared for them that love him" (Isai. 64:4; I Cor. 2:9), we can also say of Hell. It has not entered into human hearts, what is prepared for those who hate Him. Only once did Our Lord lift the veil a little bit when He told the story of Lazarus and the rich man (Luke 16:20-31). This rich man was not a criminal in our sense. He was not a murderer nor a thief. He didn't do anything especially wrong worth mentioning. But he didn't have charity. Lazarus at his doorstep was starving, and he didn't help him. He goes under the quota: "Depart from me, you cursed, into everlasting fire, which was prepared for the devil and his angels. . . . Amen, I say to you, as long as you did it not to one of these least, neither did you do it to me" (Matt. 25:41, 45).

What a terrific warning. One can go to Hell not only for what one has done, but also for what one has not done. The next thing we learn is that the rich man can look over into Heaven, where Lazarus dwells in Abraham's bosom. What must that be if the damned can perceive the blessed with the unending reproach to themselves: "There I could be now, too." Then the rich man tried to make connections and was told, "Between us and you, there is fixed a great chasm: so that they who would pass from hence to you cannot, nor from thence come hither." When the rich man pleaded that Lazarus should be allowed to bring a message to his rich brethren, he was told, "If they hear not Moses and the prophets, neither will they believe, if one rise again from the dead." Right there do we meet this *mysterium iniquitatis* again: One day Our Lord *will* rise from the dead, and so many throughout the centuries will choose not to believe.

Hell was started before the Creation of Man with that group of angels who did not want to obey: "*Non serviam!*" In their infernal hatred and jealousy, they envy every human soul the joys of Heaven, which they have voluntarily forsaken. Therefore, they are our arch-enemies. "Watch," says St. Peter (I Pet. 5:8), "because your adversary the devil, as a roaring lion goeth about seeking whom he may devour." In ancient and medieval times Satan and Hell were realities. Everybody knew about them, talked about them, and watched against them. More and more, however, has Satan and his evil spirits succeeded in our "age of enlightenment" in vanishing into a realm of myths. What grownup or, as far as that goes, what high school student, believes in a personal devil in our days? This incognito has become his strongest weapon. Behind this spiritual smoke screen he is doing untold harm, and he gets away with it unnoticed.

Every Easter Sunday we are asked by the Church, "Do you renounce Satan? And all his pomps? And all his work? We should answer, "We do renounce them."

Our Lord Himself when he allowed Satan to tempt Him, gave us an example of how to deal with our greatest enemy and remain victorious. "Begone, Satan!" (Matt. 4:10).

XXIV

"eye hath not seen"

What began with the harmless question of a little boy, "Can Martina see us now?", became a never-ending pondering of the whole family on life after death. Our initial questions were answered. Yes, Martina can see us if the rich man could see Lazarus. She does remember us and her life among us—if the rich man remembered his brothers and their way of living. As God is omnipresent—everywhere—and the souls of the blessed are in Him, isn't it very likely that they surround their beloved ones on earth, loving them more than ever before, helping them constantly with their prayers? That is why the funeral service of the Church is so consoling and uplifting: "O death, where is thy victory? O death, where is thy sting?" (I Cor. 15:55).

Also we read: "Come, ye blessed of my Father, possess you the kingdom prepared for you from the foundation of the world" (Matt. 25:34). These will be the words addressed on the last day to those who will enjoy the Beatific Vision from then on for ever and for ever. The Kingdom of Heaven! That was one of Our Lord's favorite topics. And He tried so hard to make us understand what it is like. One day, God willing, we shall find out for ourselves. Meanwhile, we have to believe St. Paul, who says, "That eye hath not seen, nor ear heard: neither hath it entered into the heart of man, what things God hath prepared for them that love him" (I Cor. 2:9; Isa. 64:4).

Even if we are warned that it hasn't entered any human heart, we can always begin to try to imagine it. We shall be united with the One "Whom our soul loveth," and this union will be more intense and more tender than any union between the most loving couple here on earth. Many times we have found out that we cannot love what we do not know. We shall know God as He is. Therefore, we shall love Him to an extent inconceivable to us now. We shall be at rest. We shall be happy. Oh—for the poverty of words! We shall be together with the Man of Nazareth, Who will recognize us as His disciples if we now patiently bear our daily cross.

"My Lord and my God" (John 20:28), we shall keep on repeating. "Rabboni! I love thee!" If in Galilee five thousand people could follow Him into the desert forgetting time and hunger because they were so fascinated by His personality, what will be in store for us when we shall see Him in His risen glory, the fairest of men, the best of friends, the most humble of all masters, He the changeless one!

We shall be united also with His mother and all His friends in a most intimate friendship. We shall be able to converse with Peter, John, Paul, Moses, Francis of Assisi and the other greats of Christianity. We shall find those millions and millions of saints, each mirroring the eternal God in another way. Then there will be the myriads of angels, not only in their nine different choirs, but each single one a spiritual world by itself; and our own Guardian Angel!

And all our friends and relatives, husbands, children, wives—will all be together—together in God! We shall remain the individuals we have been here on earth, but the possibilities which were created into us shall now find fulfillment. A scientist will know all the laws the Creator has made in nature; the historian will see in one flesh all the happenings between the first and the last day of Creation. Everything which pertains to time will be our property. We shall know it all. And nothing will any more disturb our complete one-ness with God. In Him we shall know all other things. In Him we shall meet His other children. Nothing will ever draw our attention away from Him. And all this *"sine fine"*—forever and ever, and "one day with the Lord is as a thousand years, and a thousand years as one day" (II Peter 3:8).

Yes, truly as we read these Holy Scriptures we who know Jesus as our Saviour should praise Him and leap for joy at the thought of such a glorious forever. Saint John saw in his vision the glory of Heaven and recorded it in Revelation 22:1-4, "He showed me a pure river of water of life, clear as crystal, proceeding out of the throne of God and of the Lamb. In the midst of the street of it, and on either side of the river, was there the tree of life, which bare twelve manner of fruits and yielded her fruit every month: and the leaves of the tree were for the healing of the nations. And there shall be no more curse: but the throne of God and of the Lamb shall be in it; and his servants shall serve him: and they shall see his face: and his name shall be in their foreheads. And there shall be no night there: and they need no candle, neither light of the sun; for the Lord God giveth them light: and they shall reign forever and ever."

Isn't there something to it? Doesn't it change our perspective? Measured on these giant truths, don't our petty daily troubles shrink into mere insignificance? Let us never forget that we owe it all to Him who "became partaker of our humanity that we might become partakers of His divinity," our changeless Friend, Jesus Christ, the same yesterday, today, and yes, forever.